An Unbroken Agony

HAITI, FROM REVOLUTION TO THE KIDNAPPING OF A PRESIDENT

Randall Robinson

BASIC
CIVITAS
BOOKS

A Member of the Perseus Books Group
New York

Designed by Timm Bryson

The Library of Congress has catalogued the hardcover as follows:
Robinson, Randall, 1941–
    An unbroken agony : Haiti, from revolution to the kidnapping of a president / Randall Robinson.
        p. cm.
    Includes index.
    ISBN-13: 978-0-465-07050-3
    ISBN-10: 0-465-07050-7
    1. Aristide, Jean-Bertrand. 2. Haiti--Politics and government--1986. I. Title.

F1928.23.A75R36 2007
972.9407'3--dc22

                                                          2007009753

Paperback: ISBN-13: 978-0-465-07053-4

10 9 8 7 6 5 4 3

For the indomitable Haitian people, who,
from time immemorial,
have given so much that is good to humanity,
only to receive back from it,
scarcely more than the gift of destruction.

Today we celebrate because from 1791 to 1803, our heroes, led by the revolutionary Toussaint L'Ouverture and others, dared to challenge those who had trampled on these sacred things that define our being as Africans and as human beings.

Today we are engaged in a historic struggle for the victory of the African renaissance because we are inspired by, among others, the Haitian Revolution.

We are engaged in struggle for the regeneration of all Africans, in the Americas, the Caribbean, Africa and everywhere, because we want to ensure that the struggle of our people here in Haiti, in the Caribbean, in the Americas, Europe and Africa must never be in vain.

Accordingly, together with the leadership and people of Haiti, we are determined to work together to address the problems facing this inspirational home of African freedom and achieve stability and prosperity in this important site of African heroism and wherever Africans are to be found.

We trust and are confident that in both the leadership and people of Haiti we will find equally determined partners so that together we can here, help to recreate a model country, informed by the wise words of the 1805 constitution of Haiti that we have "an opportunity of breaking our fetters, and of constituting ourselves as a people, free, civilized and independent."

In this way, we will contribute to the renaissance of Africans everywhere in the world and ensure that we are no longer an object of ridicule and pity, nor a toll of exploitation to be discarded at the fancy of the powerful, but that we become what we really and truly are: proud and confident human beings who occupy their pride of place as equals among all peoples of the world.

We wish the people of Haiti, all Africans and people of goodwill throughout the world, joyful Bicentenary Celebrations of the great Haitian Revolution whose victory was proudly proclaimed this day, January 1, two hundred years ago.

From a speech by President Thabo Mbeki of South Africa, given January 1, 2004, in Port-au-Prince, Haiti, on the occasion of the Haitian bicentennial, coming eight weeks before Haiti's president, Jean-Bertrand Aristide, and his American-born wife, Mildred Trouillot Aristide, mysteriously vanished from their country in the early morning hours of February 29, 2004.

1

Port-au-Prince, Haiti
Sunday, February 29, 2004, 4:30 A.M.

THE REAL EVENTS OF THE STORY ARE VERY UN-
like those described to the general public.

A man disappeared in the black of night from a country whose recently enfranchised poor had twice elected him to speak and act for
them. A powerful foreign enemy claimed that the man, of his own
free will, had resigned his presidency and fled for his life.

This, as it turned out, was anything but the truth.

2

The land that would later be known as Ayiti or Haiti
Sunday, December 9, 1492

Sunday, 9 December. This day it rained and the weather
was wintry as in Castile in October. . . . This island is very
big, and the Admiral says it would not be surprising if it is
two hundred leagues around. . . . This harbor at its en-
trance is a thousand pasos wide, which is a quarter of a
league. . . Facing it are some plains [vegas], the most beau-
tiful in the world, and almost like the lands of Castile;
rather these are better, for which he gave the name to the
said island la Ysla Española (Hispaniola).

CHRISTOPHER COLUMBUS
Journal of the First Voyage

IT WAS THE MOST FATEFUL OF DAYS. THE GREAT
Discoverer, Christopher Columbus, had arrived in the New

World less than two months earlier. By dint of miscalculation, the Admiral had landed not in Cipango (Japan), where he had reckoned, but in the Greater Antilles of the Caribbean archipelago.

Though the welcoming Taino Indian inhabitants of the island, by all historical accounts, intuited no danger, the European adventurer's arrival augured terrible consequences for the mild-tempered people who had lived in peace there and along a chain of neighboring islands for more than a thousand years.

Columbus's first voyage in the fall of 1492—celebrated lustily across the industrialized Western white world over the ensuing centuries—proved itself a catastrophic watershed event for Amerindians and Africans, who had been separated by a large ocean from the dawn of history. Both peoples would be painfully and irreversibly affected by forces set in motion by Columbus's Voyage of Discovery.

The Taino, in the space of a few years, all but disappeared from the face of the earth. According to researchers Woodrow Borah and Sherburne Cook of the University of California–Berkeley, on the day Columbus made landfall on Hispaniola in December 1492, an estimated 8 million Tainos were living on the island. Within twenty years there were fewer than 28,000. Thirty years on, by 1542, only two hundred Tainos remained alive.

On first sight of the island, Columbus renamed it la Ysla Española (Hispaniola), or Spanish Island, because of its resemblance to the lands of Castile.

Preoccupied by an all-consuming dream of finding gold on the island, Columbus's alter impulse, with regard to the people he had chanced upon, was to enslave them.

> Again, one is at a loss to explain why Colón (Columbus)
> would so casually assume a right to the conquest and colo-
> nialization, even the displacement and enslavement, of
> these peaceful and inoffensive people three thousand miles
> across the ocean. . . . The Admiral . . . had no difficulty in
> seeing the Tainos in this light: "They are fit to be ordered
> about and made to work, to sow and do everything else
> that may be needed" (December 16).
>
> Kirkpatrick Sale
The Conquest of Paradise

Although the Tainos had never before *seen* a European, Columbus, warped by the widespread social prejudice that marked fifteenth-century European civilization, ridiculed virtually everything he saw about them, including their inability to speak *his* language. Writes Sale, "No clothes, no arms, no possessions [Tainos were pacifistic communalists], no iron, and now no religion—not even speech: hence they were fit to be servants, and captives. It may fairly be called the birthplace of American slavery."

Within fifty years of Columbus's arrival, the Tainos and their ancient egalitarian culture had all but disappeared. Most died of diseases brought to the Americas from Europe by Columbus and his crewmen. The rest were slaughtered by the Great Discoverer, his brothers, Diego and Bartolome, Spanish colonists and soldiers armed with crossbows, pikes, lances, arguebuses, and killer dogs.

Le Cap, Haiti
Thursday, November 17, 1803

I T MAY HAVE BEEN THE MOST STUNNING VICTORY
won for the black world in a thousand years. There has been
nothing quite like it, before or since.

If the celebrated Great Discoverer, Christopher Columbus, can be
seen as opening the door to slavery in the Americas, an army of Haitian ex-slaves under the leadership of a black military genius named
Toussaint L'Ouverture, himself an ex-slave, must be credited with
setting in motion the cascading epic events that would slam the door
shut across the Americas, once and for all.

> Thus did C. L. R. James' Black Jacobins—slaves who se-
> cured their own freedom—become the most powerful sol-
> vents of the whole slave system. Only three years after
> Haitian independence, the British (and Americans) ended

their Atlantic slave trade. A generation later, the British freed all their slaves. Clearly this, and subsequent emancipations, did not derive simply from the events in Haiti. But the military and political successors of the ex-slaves in Haiti stood as a permanent rebuke to the social ideals which had shored up the slave empires of the Americas.

JAMES WALVIN

Such was the staggering global significance of the only successful slave revolt ever mounted in the Americas. As a direct result of what the Haitian revolutionaries did to free themselves, France lost two-thirds of its world trade income. Napoleon Bonaparte, with uncharacteristic despair, declared France done with empire, and a financially strapped French government offered to sell the Louisiana Territory to the United States for the bargain price of $15 million.*

In the wake of the bloody twelve-and-a-half-year revolt, thousands—French colonial officials, dispossessed white planters, middle-class free Haitian coloreds—fled St. Dominigue (Haiti) for "safety" elsewhere in the region and beyond, thus roiling slave plantations as far afield as Jamaica, Louisiana, and South Carolina.

In exchange for a commitment from the Great Liberator, Simón Bolívar, to liberate slaves in South America from Spain, a later government of the new Haitian free republic led by President Alexandre Pétion provided him not only with thousands of Haitian fighters

---

* The vast Louisiana Territory was an essential component of French Emperor Napoleon Bonaparte's imperial plans for France in the Americas. For at least two reasons, Bonaparte was loath to let it go. First, the French-held territory obstructed further westward expansion by the United States. Second, the territory produced vitally needed goods for the neighboring French slave colonies of Martinique, Guadeloupe, St. Lucia, and San Dominigue (Haiti).

and a refuge in Haiti—twice—but with "four thousand guns, fifteen thousand pounds of powder, a quantity of lead, some provisions and a printing press."

The Haitian government rolled out an unconditional welcome mat to anyone who escaped European colonialism in Africa or fled bondage from a slave plantation anywhere in the Americas, North, South, or Central.

It is not overstating to suggest that across the globe the Haitian revolutionaries with their magnificent victory had, to paraphrase Martinican writer Frantz Fanon, "set afoot" a *new* black woman, man, child. A shimmering new pulsating consciousness of tangible, embraceable possibility. The days of involuntary servitude were, at long last, numbered. Most everyone everywhere—enslaved and enslaver alike—recognized that the countdown to slavery's end (which would finally exhaust itself in the final stages of the American Civil War) had been set ticking by the Haitian, Toussaint L'Ouverture, and his triumphant army of ex-slaves.

The slave revolt began in August 1791, two years after the the French Revolution started. The social tumult in France disturbed the volatile chemistry in the French slave colonies abroad, where whites and free mulattoes, rich and middle class, expatriates and colony-born colonials, coexisted in an unstable state of sufferance that was rife with mutual suspicion.

As the privileged classes quarreled among themselves, the slaves revolted—first in the north of St. Dominigue and then, within weeks, across the full face of the colony with 40,000 of the colony's 465,429 slaves quickly joining the ranks of the rebellion.

By turn, black armies led by L'Ouverture and Jean-Jacques Dessalines (like L'Ouverture, an ex-slave) overran the French plantocratic edifice and then thrashed an invading opportunistic Spanish force, followed by two armies of 60,000 professional soldiers each that had been dispatched from Britain and Napoleon's new France to quell the revolt.

Over the course of the long war, American support for the French slave system in St. Dominigue remained consistently strong.

As the slave rebellion progressed, Thomas Jefferson, a slave owner himself, said, "If this combustion can be introduced among us under any veil whatever, we have to fear it." Jefferson, writing to the French minister in America, Louis André Pinchon, about revolt leader Toussaint L'Ouverture, hinted menacingly that "nothing would be easier than to furnish your army and fleet with everything, and reduce Toussaint to starvation." George Washington later added that it was "lamentable to see such a spirit of revolution among the blacks" of Saint Domingue. But American support for slavery in St. Dominigue figured little in the final outcome.

On January 1, 1804, the same day that French soldiers sailed for France in humiliating defeat, Dessalines proclaimed his country a free and independent republic, severed its ties with France, and gave the land that had been called *St. Domingue* a new name, *Haiti.* Dessalines is then said to have torn the color white from the French tricolor flag, leaving in place the red and blue. He then replaced the letters *R.F.*, standing for Republic of France, with the new words *Liberty or Death.*

Garry Wills in *Negro President* writes of the American reaction:

> From that moment, Jefferson and the Republicans showed nothing but hostility to the new nation. Already in 1802, Jefferson had expressed his continued concern over black rebellion to Rufus King, lamenting that the "course of

things in the neighboring islands of the West Indies appeared to have given a considerable impulse to the minds of the slaves" in the United States and "a great disposition to the insurgency has manifested itself among them." When he proposed an embargo of the island . . . Republicans in Congress welcomed this as a great opportunity. . . . Jefferson refused to grant diplomatic recognition to the new nation of Haiti, though this went against the clear norms he had earlier established for granting such recognition. As secretary of state in 1792, he defended the recognition of the revolutionary French government: "We certainly cannot deny to other nations that principle whereon our own government is founded, that every nation had a right to govern itself internally under what forms it please, and to, change those forms at its own will."

By the late eighteenth century, the French slave colony of St. Dominigue had eclipsed Jamaica as the most profitable slave colony in the world. By then, owing to its composition and the brutally harsh treatment the French accorded its slave labor force, the colony was growing dangerously unstable.

Most have assumed that (Haiti's) slaves had no military experience prior to the revolution. Many assume that they rose from agricultural labor to military prowess in an amazingly short time. . . . However, it is probably a mistake to see the slaves of St. Domingue as simply agricultural workers, like the peasants of Europe. . . . A majority of St. Domingue's slaves, especially those who fought steadily in the revolution were born in Africa. . . . In fact, a great many had served in African armies prior to their enslavement and arrival in Haiti. . . . Sixty to seventy percent of the adult slaves listed on (St. Domingue's) inventories in the late 1780's and 1790's were African born. . . .

Where the African military background of the slaves counted most was in those areas, especially in the north (of St. Domingue), where slaves themselves led the revolution, both politically and militarily. . . These areas. . . threw up the powerful armies of Toussaint L'Ouverture and Dessalines and eventually carried the revolution.

John K. Thornton
African Soldiers in the Haitian Revolution

French plantation managers behaved bestially toward the largely African-born population of slaves that toiled in St. Dominigue under a broiling sun an average of fifteen hours a day, likely contributing to France's ultimate undoing. Slaves were routinely worked to death, starved to death, or beaten to death with a cane or a *rigoise* (a thick thong of cowhide).

It is not known whether the battle fought on the morning of November 16, 1803, at Le Cap was the last battle of the war or even the penultimate battle. It is very well established, however, that it was the *decisive* battle, the battle that gave a half-million black Haitian slaves their freedom, that triggered events that would herald the final stages of slavery in the whole of the Western Hemisphere, and, with the same stroke, dash, once and for all, Napoleon Bonaparte's grand dreams of world empire.

Reports on the famous battle were that, under blistering fire from French muskets and heavy-gauge artillery pieces, Capois Death, a black officer leading a column of ex-slave soldiers, shouted above the concussive blasts, "En avant! En avant!" *Forward! Forward!* as, mounted, he hurled himself and his men against the French line of fire in an assault on the blockhouses of Bréda and Champlin. Demonstrating the bravery that gave him his nom de guerre, Death, he then rode at full gallop toward the French fort at Vertieres. When his horse was shot from under him, he rose and charged afoot to-ward the thick walls of the fort, pointing his sword in the direction of the French guns mounted behind the parapet, crying out anew to his men, "En avant! En avant!" His hat was then shot from his head. Again, he charged the French guns that exploded the ground around him. Men fell gut-shot, blood all about. The sounds, sight, and smell of the awful deaths mixed with peals of thundering ordnance.

"En avant! En avant!" Death screamed, afoot still, never slowing.

It was the battle that turned the war and handed victory to an army of ex-slaves who'd soundly defeated three of the very best of Europe's armies.

Of the more than 465,000 black slaves living in Haiti when the re-volt began, 150,000 would die during twelve and a half years of fight-ing for their freedom.

A half century after the revolution, Frenchman Lemonier-Delafosse, who avidly supported Haitian slavery, wrote of the black revolution-aries in his memoirs: "But what men these blacks are! How they fight and how they die! One has to make war against them to know their reckless courage in braving danger. . . I have seen a solid column, torn by grape-shot from four pieces of cannon, advance without making a retrograde step. The more they fell, the greater seemed to be the courage of the rest."

How did a force of ill-equipped ex-slaves defeat the best that Eu-rope could muster against it? Why did the rebellion occur in Haiti and not in another French slave colony? How were Haitian blacks different from the blacks in Guadeloupe or St. Lucia or Martinique, the birthplace of Napoleon's wife, Josephine?

First, many Haitians had been soldiers in an Africa that they remembered well. The ever avaricious French had expanded the captured Africans' numbers in Haiti so rapidly as to drive them well beyond the colonists' ability to forcibly reacculturate them. As a result, the newly arrived Africans developed (or retained in critical mass) African memories, mores, and behaviors that tied them more closely together than enslaved Africans may have been in other French colonies. For instance, the Haitian slaves largely retained or adapted the African religions of their birth. By the close of slavery, Haitian Kreyol was distinguishable from the Kreyol spoken in St. Lucia, Guadeloupe, and Martinique. Haitian Kreyol was more redolently *African* and less *French*-laden than the Kreyol spoken in the other French slave possessions. Further, French slavery in Haiti was not only the most profitable worldwide for the French but also the most cruel.

They were about a hundred men and women of different ages, all occupied in digging ditches in a cane-field, the majority of them naked or covered with rags. The sun shone down with full force on their heads. Sweat rolled from all parts of their bodies. Their limbs, weighed down by the heat, fatigued with the weight of their picks and by the resistance of the clayey soil baked hard enough to break their implements, strained themselves to overcome every obstacle. A mournful silence reigned. Exhaustion was stamped on every face, but the hour of rest had not yet come. The pitiless eye of the Manager patrolled the gangs and several

foremen armed with long whips moved periodically between them, giving stinging blows to all who, worn out by
fatigue, were compelled to take rest—men or women,
young or old.

GIROD-CHANTRANS
Voyage d'un Suisse en différentes colonies, Neufchâtel, 1785

In fields like these, Haitian slaves fell dead by the thousands.
Many who survived the savage work conditions were slaughtered
episodically by the French for the amusement of spectators. The
French general Donatien Rochambeau routinely massacred large
numbers of blacks in public square killings and drownings. On one
occasion, he ordered his soldiers to

"draw some blood. That'll get them (dogs) started" and
men with bayonets went out, protecting themselves from
the dogs who wanted to attack them and not the blacks,
and jabbed at the bellies of the three blacks until blood
spurted, whereupon the dogs leaped at the men, tore them
apart, and devoured them. The audience applauded.

JAMES A. MICHENER
Caribbean

Claude Ribbe, a French human rights commissioner and noted
historian, reports in his book *The Crime of Napoleon* that the French
emperor Napoleon Bonaparte carried out a campaign of genocide
against the rebellious Haitian slaves by gassing them.

In response to the slaves' quest for their freedom, Napoleon ordered the extermination of all Haitian blacks over the age of twelve.

Many of the victims were gassed to death in ships' holds with sulphur dioxide before Napoleon's humiliating defeat at the hands of Toussaint's and Dessalines's armies.

On an unprecedented scale, the French murdered and worked the colony's African slaves to death by the tens of thousands, and replaced them in waves with fresh captives from Africa. Many, if not most, of those captured had been soldiers in African armies. Some who became fierce fighters in the slave rebellion had been brought to Haiti from other Caribbean slave colonies—men like the storied Boukman from Jamaica and the legendary Makandal from Trinidad and the great general, Henri Christophe, who was born in Grenada and is believed to have lived for a period in St. Kitts.* After the slave revolt got under way, an indeterminate number of blacks fleeing slavery in America made their way to Haiti to fight in the revolution.

Lastly, the world's only successful slave revolt was accomplished in Haiti, in no small part, because Haitian slaves were blessed with an accident of leadership genius in the special gifts of L'Ouverture and Dessalines, generals who worked well together though diametrically dissimilar in personality and philosophy.

L'Ouverture had been the rigorous intellectual, the African humanist, the military strategist, the administrator and, not insignificantly, the conciliator. Less nuanced of personality than L'Ouverture, Dessalines had been, first and last, the hard-nosed soldier who believed that an enemy as manifestly unsalvageable as the French had to be, wherever possible, obliterated.

* In 1779, twelve years before the start of the Haitian revolution, Henri Christophe at the age of twelve fought alongside the soldiers of George Washington with a group of eight hundred Haitian blacks and mulattoes in the American Revolution at the Battle of Savannah, where Haitians died in the cause of American independence.

While the Haitians owed their successful revolution to both men, they owed their keen sense of African ethos and tradition largely to L'Ouverture, who was the ceaseless shaper of a shared self-owned black consciousness.

4

Haiti
1805

ARLY IN THE LIFE OF THE NEW FREE HAITIAN republic, conditions imposed on it from outside greatly constricted the public policy choices available to the leaders of the first nation in the world to abolish slavery completely. Even before France leveraged the weak new state with crushing financial reparations in 1825, the United States and western Europe—including the Vatican—moved on the heels of the French army's infelicitous departure in 1804 to cripple the fledgling nation socially, politically, and economically, just as France was fashioning new policies to favor Haiti's minority community of French white ex-colonists and mulattoes, the people in Haiti who needed French help least.

Unsurprisingly, the black peasant community—impoverished by centuries of French slavery and devastated by the war that ended it— found itself in a state of perilous social disrepair. Unlike the fair-skinned Haitians who always had a monopoly on education, education by the early 1800s was a privilege rarely enjoyed by blacks. French abolitionist Victor Schoelcher estimated that of a postwar population of 700,000 Haitian black children, only one thousand were allowed to attend school.

The Vatican had an avid hand in this discrimination, refusing to recognize the new republic until fifty-six years after its founding.

Haitian historian Michel-Rolph Trouillot describes the consequence to the fledgling republic of the Vatican's isolation:

> In Catholic Europe as in the current and former colonies of Catholic nations, religious orders have always been the backbone of the formal education system. Starting from scratch, with a population just liberated from slavery, Haiti badly needed the help that the missionaries could have provided. St. Dominigue never had a formal educational system, of course, and only a few of the richer mulattoes had been schooled in Europe. Both (Alexandre) Pétion (in the south) and (Henri) Christophe (in the north) had established primary schools in the areas they controlled, but those institutions were aimed primarily at the urban elite. By the time church-schools were finally created, after the 1860 Concordat in which the Vatican formally recognized Haiti, these urban elites had already tuned the education system so that it would serve their needs exclusively.

Though Article 19 of the Haitian constitution of 1805 called for a public school in every military division of the country, the government (or governments: one in the north and one in the south) had few resources it could use to offset the concentration of public schools in the cities, even though 90 percent of the population lived in the countryside. What few public resources the government did manage to control, it quite reasonably applied to the needs of the military.

> As late as 1822 such concerns were not unfounded. The party of former French colonists remained armed and had political support in France. Two years later in the United States, where slavery was still lawful, a senator declared: "Our policy with regard to Haiti is plain. We never can acknowledge her independence. . . . The peace and safety of a large portion of the union forbids us to ever discuss it." Some U.S. statesmen persisted in referring to the Haitians as "rebel slaves."
>
> MILDRED ARISTIDE
> *Child Domestic Service in Haiti and*
> *Its Historical Underpinnings*

Though the revolution itself had been a singular achievement, the United States, France and western Europe would quickly join together in a program of measures designed to defeat the new black republic's prospects for success. For the next two hundred years, Haiti would be faced with active hostility from the world's most powerful community of nations. The new country endured a variety of attacks, some imposed concurrently, others consecutively, including military invasions, economic embargoes, gunboat blockades, reparations demands, trade barriers, diplomatic quarantines, subsidized armed subversions, media volleys of public traducement, and a string of twentieth-century U.S.-armed black dictators, beginning with

François (Papa Doc) Duvalier, who rose to power in 1957 and was succeeded by his son, Jean-Claude (Baby Doc) Duvalier in 1971. Jean-Claude Duvalier in turn was followed by a similarly cruel and uncivil line of petty despots—Henri Namphy (who would rule twice), Lesli Manigat, and Prosper Avril.

5

As punishment for creating the first free republic in the Americas (when 13 percent of the people living in the United States were slaves), the new Republic of Haiti was met with a global economic embargo imposed by the United States and Europe. The embargo was strengthened by a further demand from France for financial reparations of roughly $21 billion (2004 dollars) as compensation from the newly freed slaves for denying France the further benefit of owning them. It would be the first time in history that reparations would be imposed by a defeated nation on the nation that had defeated it.

American economic sanctions against Haiti would not end until the Emancipation Proclamation in 1863, nearly sixty years after the founding of the free Haitian republic.

In 1825, twenty-two years after L'Ouverture's death, the Haitian army was no longer the feared fighting force it had once been. France, threatening to reenslave Haitians, imposed an ordinance requiring from Haiti a payment of 150 million francs and a 50 percent tariff reduction for all French ships docking in Haiti.* To meet the first payment of 30 million francs under the terms of the ordinance, the government of Haiti was constrained to borrow the full amount from a private French bank, MM Ch Ternaux Grandolphe et Cie.

After extended negotiations, in 1838, under the Traité d'Amitié (Treaty of Friendship), the original obligation of 150 million francs was reduced to 90 million francs, with the government of Haiti required to make thirty annual payments of 2 million francs in order to pay off the 60 million franc balance. Haiti had to make these payments in addition to payments it had been making to a succession of private banks from which it had to borrow at onerous interest rates in order to meet the terms of its original unjust obligation to France.

> And forcing slaves who had won their freedom to compensate their former masters for their lost property was recognized, even in the 19th century, as a violation of human rights and international laws. By the time of the 1825 Ordinance, the international slave trade had been abolished and the reintroduction of slavery into free territories forbidden by the Second Treaty of Paris and the Congress of Vienna—both of which France had signed in 1815.
>
> *Human Rights Advocates*

* From a statement by Human Rights Advocates, an American organization that supports efforts to win restitution from France for the Haitian people: "Compare the (French-) imposed cost of Haiti's independence—150,000,000 francs—to the price paid by the United States to France for the Louisiana purchase—80,000,000 francs for an area of land seventy-four times that of Haiti and one can only begin to sense the enormity of the reparations burden and the extortionate terms imposed."

As late as 1915, 111 years after the successful slave revolt, some 80 percent of the Haitian government's resources were being paid out in debt service to French and American banks on loans that had been made to enable Haiti to pay reparations to France.

In 1922, seven years into a nineteen-year American military occupation of Haiti that resulted in 15,000 Haitian deaths, the United States imposed a $16 million loan on the Haitian government to pay off its "debt" to France.

The American loan was finally paid off in 1947. Haiti was left virtually bankrupt, its workforce in desperate straits.

The Haitian economy has never recovered from the financial havoc France (and America) wreaked upon it, during and after slavery.

6

THE VICTORY THAT HAITIAN SLAVES WON OVER
France's largest-ever naval task force commanded by General
Charles Leclerc, the brother-in-law of Napoleon Bonaparte, is the
most important event in the history of black Kreyol-speaking
Haitians. It is therefore not surprising that contemporary Kreyol-
speaking Haitians—blacks, rural peasants, *moun andeyo* (people from
outside the cities)—would retain more from Africa's rich cultural
palette in their social practices than do virtually any other of Africa's
descendant progeny living in the Americas.

Africa can be heard in their music. It can be felt stirring in their religion, Voudou, which is African in its origins. Africa is spiritually recalled in Haitian paintings in the form of wildlife, representing, not
Haiti, but the Guinea to which black Haitians, whose forbears were
wrenched from their homeland by slavers, believe that in death they
will one day return. Africa can be heard in the ordinary Haitian
Kreyol social remark, *Ou se yon bon nèg ginen*, which means *you are a*

good African or, less literally, *you are a good person.* (Haiti is the only country in the world outside Africa where this expression is in common use.)

Unlike blacks in North America and the Caribbean generally, Haitians have proverbs, hundreds of them, if not thousands. The ancient stored social wisdom of Africa antedating the North Atlantic slave trade survives virtually intact in Haiti.

An ancient African proverb tells that "The ax forgets but not the tree." The same proverb's linear diasporic descendant is Haitian: *Bay kou bliye, pote mak sonje.* "Those who give the blows forget; those who bear the scars remember."

Deeply interwoven in the modern Haitian subconscious are themes of origin, the middle passage, the heroic revolution, and the terrible price black Haitians were forced to pay for it by a white world that has never forgotten or forgiven it. Indeed, it can scarcely be gainsaid that the poorest black Haitians' tenacious, relentless memory has caused France, America, and the white world in general to resent and malign them.

The evidence of this unflagging polarity is both figurative and literal.

Christopher Columbus remains a revered figure throughout Europe, the United States, and the Dominican Republic. Among black Haitians, however, Columbus is broadly viewed as the founding father of the North Atlantic slave trade, whose trade missions across the Caribbean resulted in decimation for the indigenous Amerindians who had been living there for thousands of years, and in slavery on an industrial scale for Africans who had been captured and brought across the Atlantic Ocean to toil and die in bondage.

After the dictator Jean-Claude (Baby Doc) Duvalier fled the country in February 1986, a crowd of Haitian demonstrators tore a statue of Columbus from its Port-au-Prince base in Bicentenaire, carted it off, and threw it into the Caribbean Sea. The statue was never recovered. The Haitian public renamed the site in honor of Charlemagne Péralte, the black peasant farmer who in 1917 raised an army of peasant farmers, the Cacos soldiers, to fight against the American marines who were then occupying the country.

Why would Americans not look on this self-affirming act as the Haitian equivalent of America's Boston Tea Party? The answer, put simply, is *race*.

From Thomas Jefferson onward, race largely explains the conspicuously historic, if unconscious, American affinity for rigidly antidemocratic forces in Haiti, forces that, to the present day, comprise the white and mixed-race business class, the inveterate Francophiles who spit the word *diaspopo* (a corruption of diaspora) when referring to poor black Haitians and the camouflaging black mercenaries with whom the elites enjoy a mutually beneficial understanding. Lastly, there is America's peculiarly intense and age-old animus toward black Haitians—a compulsive contorting undertow of prejudice whose ruinous power measures inversely to the pride Haitians take in having been the only black military force in world history to rout and humiliate the best of Europe's armies.

> By a phenomenon often observed, the individual leadership responsible for the unique achievement was almost the work of a single man—Toussaint L'Ouverture. . . . The writer believes that between 1789 and 1815 with the single exception of Bonaparte himself, no single figure appeared on the historical stage more greatly gifted than this Negro, a slave till he was forty-five.
>
> C. L. R. JAMES
> *The Black Jacobins*

Thus one can easily understand what all the fuss surrounding L'Ouverture and his stunning achievement is quite deservedly about. Neither L'Ouverture nor his rebellion, however, are familiar today to most Americans, sadly, not even African Americans.

Oblivion for the undeserving is rarely an accident.

In 1904, Haiti invited France to celebrate the centennial of Haitian freedom but it declined the invitation, responding that it would reconsider that request in one hundred years.

In 2003, the president of one of Africa's most influential countries raised the subject of Haiti's approaching bicentennial celebrations in a meeting with French President Jacques Chirac. Chirac replied dryly that he did not like the sitting president of Haiti.

Shadowed by a long past of cruel experiences, contemporary Haitians have ample reason to believe that where the world's white nations are concerned, notions of democracy and other abstract decencies weigh little against the ageless and seductive traditions of color prejudice and greed. The leaders of the white world simply do not accord to the constitutions and laws of black countries the near sanctity they accord to their own. They value the written compacts that bind black nations little more than they do the paper the compacts are printed on, and even less so when such documents (which are vital for any new national society's constancy) pose a hindrance to the strategies and interests of the world's powerful community of historically compulsive interlopers.

7

A DARK SOUL EMBOLDENED BY PRIDE OR VIRTUE, who elects to retrieve a stolen birthright, resist a cruel domination, or militantly ward away the puissant swarming spores of Columbus and his like, must decide at some point to engage the silver-tongued takers to draw them into a dangerous intimacy and, by so engaging them, risk a contagion of the spirit, or fates even worst.

The odds of success are never good. The taker controls all but the most abstract and otherwise valueless of weapons. For it is always the taker who controls the gun, the wealth, the heralds of public information, and more often than not the weak's very own thoughts.

The rebellious dark soul controls only the small candle of an ageless ideal, a faint but unyielding flame guttering low beneath a fierce foreign storm that would seem more powerful than the dark soul's sturdy ideal, but younger still by an eternity than the taker's all-consuming greed, which never seems to abate.

When President Jean-Bertrand Aristide and his wife disappeared on February 29, 2004, nearly two hundred years and two months after Jean-Jacques Dessalines declared Haiti a free and independent republic, 1 percent of the country's people held 50 percent of the country's wealth. Slavery had long since ended, but the country's wealth remained concentrated in the closed fists of the very few whose families and descendants had seized and held onto it since the early 1700s.

Into this harsh social landscape of intractable economic and political inequity, Jean-Bertrand Aristide was born poor and black in July 1953 in Port Salut, a tiny rural hamlet in the south of Haiti. His mother, Solange Pierre Louis Aristide, was a *commercante*, or one who bought and sold things—fabrics, food, and the like. His father, Joseph S. Aristide, died when his son was three months old. Aristide's mother was born in Carpentier, a small district just outside Port Salut that was at the top of a mountain. This was where the young Jean-Bertrand and his sister, who was two years his senior, went in summer to be near their maternal grandfather, Pierre Louis, a poor but estimable man who figured as a large influence in the formation of his young grandson's values.

The young president-to-be earned a degree in philosophy and his *license* in psychology at the State University of Haiti. Though none of Haiti's elites would have considered sending their children to a university in Haiti, Aristide so distinguished himself there academically that he was subsequently permitted to study biblical theology in Israel. Returning to Haiti, he was ordained a Catholic priest on July 3, 1982. Later he studied at the University of Montreal, where he completed his master's degree in biblical theology. Returning to Haiti, he taught Hebrew, theology, and psychology and completed his dissertation for a Ph.D. in theology.

In response to young Father Aristide's rousing church sermons opposing the brutal rule of Jean-Claude Duvalier and the repressive military juntas that followed, his church, St. Jean Bosco, was attacked and burned to the ground on September 11, 1988, as the future president celebrated mass. Dozens of parishioners were killed. The assailants directed a fusillade of rounds at the priest as he stood looking calmly into their faces. None of the shots fired at close range struck him. He was said to have already survived nine attempts on his life by partisans of the junta.

Father Aristide's Sunday masses were attended by thousands of the Haitian black poor who lived in nearby La Saline, one of the largest slums in the capital. His sermons were broadcast across the country on Radio Soleil, Catholic Church radio. The slightly built priest would remind his parishioners of the Haitian proverb *Tout moun se moun* (every human being is a human being), instantly transforming the debilitating pain of his individual parishioners into a galvanizing new summons to purpose for millions of the poor. Among a privileged minority of Haitians and non-Haitians made nervous by the transformational effect the priest's Sunday sermons had on the poor was the Vatican, which, with a touch of irony, expelled Aristide from the Salesian Order on the grounds that his advocacy on behalf of the destitute and voiceless had, in the fashion of Christ, crossed over from religion to politics.

In temperament, intellect, and political philosophy, Aristide, the ethical democrat whom the Americans and the French would later judge unpalatable, appeared a lineal disciple of L'Ouverture.

A story is told that during the fighting, ex-slave revolutionary soldiers delivered two captured French colonists to L'Ouverture and asked him what to do with them. L'Ouverture is said to have scooped up in one hand several dark stones and in the other hand a number of light stones. Looking at his soldiers, he mixed the stones together. *Let them live.*

From the beginning of his rise to power, Aristide would say, "Our vision relates to life, not to death. We always thought we had to use the judicial system and not guns. We had taken and stayed on a moral line. After all, our enemies had more guns than we anyway."

By the late 1980s, with the country under the bloody fist of General Prosper Avril, Aristide, then a young parish priest, had emerged to outsiders as the most visible face of the newly organized Haitian poor. The young priest, however, never envisioned himself or his role in messianic terms:

> The emergence of the people as an organized public force, as a collective consciousness, was already taking place in Haiti in the 1980's, and by 1986 this force was strong enough to push the Duvalier dictatorship from power. It was a grassroots popular movement, and not at all a top-down project driven by a single leader of a single organization. It wasn't an exclusively political movement, either. It took shape, above all, through the constitution, all over the country, in many small church communities or *ti legliz.* It was these small communities that played the decisive historical role. When I was elected President, it wasn't strictly a political affair, it wasn't the election of a politician, of a conventional political party. No, it was an ex-

pression of a broad popular movement, of the mobilization of the people as a whole. For the first time, the national palace became a place not just for professional politicians, but for the people themselves. The simple fact of allowing ordinary people to enter the palace, the simple fact of welcoming people from the poorest sections of Haitian society within the very center of traditional power—this was a profoundly transformative gesture.

It was left to the revered elderly Catholic bishop from Jérémie, Monsignor Wily Romélus, to come to Aristide in 1990 well after a full slate of candidates had declared for the country's first ever democratic presidential election. The monsignor told Aristide that he, Father Antoine Adrien, and many others in the popular movement were asking him to "accept the cross that had fallen to him."

Initially Aristide refused. But the monsignor insisted, "You are on the road to Calvary." When Aristide appeared reluctant still, Monsignor Romélus asserted that the young priest had little choice.

"Your life doesn't belong to you anymore," the monsignor said, "You have given it as a sacrifice for the people. And now that a concrete obligation has fallen on you, now that you are faced with this particular call to follow Jesus and take up the cross, think carefully before you turn your back on it."

A few days before the December 1990 election that made him Haiti's first democratically elected president, Aristide attended a service to commemorate the victims of the Ruelle Vaillant massacre of November 29, 1987. Ton Ton Macoutes slaughtered twenty people that day in an effort to force a cancellation of elections.

At the commemoration service, a student asked Aristide, "Father, do you think that by yourself you'll be able to change this situation, which is so corrupt and unjust?"

Aristide answered, "In order for it to rain do you need one or many drops? In order to have a flood, do you need a trickle of water or a river in spate?"

Later, Aristide remembered the exchange with the young man. "I thanked him for giving me the chance to present our collective mission in the form of this metaphor: it is not alone, as isolated drops of water, that you or I are going to change the situation, but together, as a flood or torrent, *lavalassement*, that we are going to change it, to clean things up without any illusions that it would be easy or quick."

8

Port-au-Prince
Friday, July 5, 2002, 3:00 A.M.

ATTEMPTS BY BLACK REBELS—TACITLY EN-
dorsed by the business class—to overthrow the government
had come in waves over a number of months.

In their first major insurrectionary incident, a rebel force made up
of former members of the country's disbanded army on July 5, 2002,
attacked the Police Academy and School of Magistrature on Route
de Frères in Port-au-Prince, a ten-minute drive from the president's
home at Tabarre, just outside the city.

The rebels killed five Haitian police officers during the attack that
night and kidnapped a woman who was later released. The assault
was mounted by uniformed men answerable to Guy Philippe, a former police precinct captain of the Delmas district of Port-au-Prince.
As a policeman, Philippe had been selected by the Central Intelligence Agency for military training in Ecuador.

Having little choice but to dissolve the corrupt, brutal army with Duvalierist roots, President Jean-Bertrand Aristide knew that the government could not rely solely on the ill-equipped, lightly trained, and poorly paid Haitian police force to defend it against the rebels, many of whom were known to have committed grisly human rights crimes.* Though vastly better equipped than the police, the rebels, who werze relatively small in number, enjoyed virtually no support from the general public.

Before this, the first of several violent rebel forays into the capital, both the government and the rebels knew that that the attackers, while able to demonstrate short, spectacular displays of superior fire-power, had no ability to topple the government or even sustain more than a brief presence against the overwhelming weight of a demon-strative general public that had come to relish the democracy whose most basic rights it had only recently begun to exercise.

In any case, the purpose of the raid on the Police Academy was never to take and hold the sprawling low-walled facility, as it was to draw public attention to the rebels themselves.

In the middle of the night, fifty rebels, fitted out in new gear and battle greens, brandishing M16 rifles, scaled the short wall of the fa-cility that was once Haiti's military academy. Having trained on the

---

* Just before the coup, the country had a police force of three thousand officers with three hundred deployed in the Port-au-Prince area to protect the capital of 1 million people. The officers were equipped with six-round 38 millimeter duty revolvers and a few rounds of ammo. The revolvers and the bullets were old and unreliable. The officers were largely without radios and transportation. The sixty small Nissans donated by Taiwan were not suitable for Haiti's pitted roads and most were discarded within a year at a junkyard near the airport. On special occasions, the police rented SUVs from local car rental companies. The average salary for a police officer was $250 a month. A precinct captain made about $800 a month.

grounds for the old Haitian army, the rebels had little difficulty finding and then surrounding the barracks that housed Haiti's special unit SWAT team of fifty police officers. As the officers slept, the rebels opened fire on the building. The thick wooden door in the front of the structure was blown inward and off its hinges by a projectile from a rebel grenade launcher.

Five sleeping police officers were slain before others woke to return the rebels' fire. Help arrived shortly as SWAT team members ran across the grounds from their assigned duty posts firing MP5s, a German-made submachine gun. Within minutes, the rebels melted into the night to begin the long truck ride east to the rebel camp across the border in the Dominican Republic.

One rebel lay dead with his American-made M16 on the ground beside him.

On July 10, 2002, the government held a national funeral for the five dead police officers at the national police academy.

A government plainclothes security officer who came to the site just after the attack had once served in the U.S. Army. After examining the body and the weapon of the dead rebel, he reported to his superiors that the weapon found beside the body was identical to the weapon he had used when he served in the American army. The officer further reported that absent the shoulder unit patch and the name tag above the breast pocket, the new olive drab fatigue field uniform worn by the dead rebel was identical to the uniforms worn by American infantrymen. He surmised that the grenade fragments found inside the damaged barracks had come from the same source as well.

Though dismayed, President Aristide was not surprised by the security officer's report. Dating back to Haiti's successful slave rebellion against France, which culminated in the world's first free black re-public in 1804, no historian or scholar of consequence ever docu-mented a single meaningful instance of official American sympathy for Haiti's long oppressed black poor.

● ● ●

The Haitian "rebels" who attacked the police academy in 2002 were cashiered thugs with a string of brutal killings to their credit. They had no visible means of support or employment. Where had they ob-tained the state-of-the-art American arms, ammunition, and equip-ment—matériel that the Haitian government could ill afford? It almost certainly had been passed on to them by the government of the Dominican Republic, which just as certainly would not have passed it along without an express order from Washington.

The Dominican Republic had long enjoyed a warm working rela-tionship with the United States. Conversely, the tension that histori-cally had exacerbated relations between Haiti and its neighbor appeared as fixed in place as the River Massacre. The river divides the two countries and takes its name from the 1937 massacre of 35,000 Haitians by Dominican dictator Rafael Trujillo. After the massacre, the American secretary of state, Cordell Hull, is remembered to have remarked that "Trujillo is one of the greatest men in Central America and in most of South America."

9

T HE COLOR PROBLEM IN HAITI DATES AS FAR
back as the December 9, 1492, arrival of Christopher Columbus. More than three hundred years thence, the problem would over-
whelm and survive, undiminished, the establishment of the world's
first black republic in 1804. In the minds of the color-privileged, little
in Haiti has changed in the two centuries that followed the republic's founding. The United States, France, and western Europe continue to play the unconstructive roles they have always played. In
Haiti today, color remains as insuperable a barrier to social progress
as ever.

. . . despite these rebuffs, the mulatto proprietors remained
on the whole uneasily pro-British. Whenever Toussaint
captured an area, following his usual policy, he welcomed
them if they took the oath of allegiance to the Republic.

But as soon as his back was turned, they would intrigue
and plot to get the British back. . . .

The mulattoes felt that they could govern the country
themselves, they were aiming at independence and some of
the local whites conspired with them. These mulatto citizens . . . wish to enjoy everything themselves. The mulattoes and former free blacks of Le Cap could not bear to see
ex-slaves do well in business or hold any position.

C. L. R. JAMES

The Black Jacobins

Not even the least controversial of President Aristide's proposed
social reforms were conceded by his lighter-skinned and more privileged fellow citizens. Not even his proposal to strike the word *peasant*
as a category of citizenship from the national birth certificate form
that all rural blacks bore. This idea of his caused more than a few of
Haiti's powerful elites to intensify their dislike for him.

Before he was elected the first time in 1990, Haiti had two cate-
gories of citizenship, with one or the other kind indelibly noted at
birth on a newborn's birth certificate.

The first category was described in law to include those who enjoyed certain basic unencumbered rights of conventional citizenship,
not unlike those enjoyed by people living elsewhere in the region. In
Haiti this category traditionally was reserved for whites, mulattoes,
and the city-born of means.

The second category of citizenship was reserved for Haitians born
in the countryside. Reserved, de facto, for poor blacks (the majority
of Haiti's people, including the president, who had been born poor in
rural Port Salut), the birth certificate issued to the people in this cat-

egory was stamped at the top with the Kreyol* words *peyizan*, for peasant, and *moun andeyo*, for people from outside.†

The president saw the birth certificate as the kind of culturally engrained race-based discrimination that encouraged, among other indignities, the common practice of whites gratuitously whipping poor black children unmercifully, as if they were issue of an unrelated species.

Thus in an early act of office, the president signed a decree in 1991 requiring a common birth certificate form for all Haitians. But the coup d'état of September 30, 1991, occurred before the parliament could pass a law supporting the decree.

That the president, who was fluent in at least eight languages, was indisputably brilliant made little difference to his detractors, who, in any case, chose to see themselves as more French than Haitian. Those who, within earshot of their black servants, casually disparaged blacks as *bête* or *stupid beasts* or *yon Kongo*, saw little difference between the blacks they disparaged and the exquisitely well-mannered man the country twice elected as president.

Decades before, the poet Langston Hughes, with aggrieved disappointment, had written of the Haitian mixed-race bourgeoisie's attitude toward the black underclass:

> It was in Haiti that I first realized how class lines may cut across color lines within a race, and how dark people of the same nationality may scorn those below them. Certainly

---

* *Kreyol* is the correct Haitian language spelling for the word that non-Haitians spell as *Creole*.

† Haitian anthropologist Michel-Rolph Trouillot concluded in a study that "in Haiti, the peasantry is the nation."

the upper-class Haitians I observed at a distance seemed a delightful and cultured group. No doubt, many of the French slave owners were delightful and cultured too— but the slaves could not enjoy their culture.

Coming from America, Hughes would likely not have understood that Haiti's lighter-skinned and more privileged "blacks" virtually saw themselves as members of a race apart from the large majority of the Haitian people who were darker and poorer than they.

Even now (though it would be sharply more the case in Haiti), race lines in the Caribbean generally are marked off somewhat differently than they are in America, where "blacks," who are grouped together as a single race, come in limitless shades owing to the miscegenational assault by a comparatively larger number of whites during the long and more recent years of American slavery. As a result, Caribbean blacks are visibly less mixed than are blacks in America, and light-skinned blacks in the Caribbean who look, for instance, like Langston Hughes, are often assessed by locals to be something other than black.

A light-skinned African American stood in an ATM line not long ago in downtown Basseterre, St. Kitts, where I live. When he was distracted by someone calling out a greeting to him, a gap opened in the line in front of him. Unaware that the African American was in the line, a Kittitian joining what he thought was the end of the line moved in front of the African American. The Kittitian's friend, who was standing nearby and had seen what had happened, said to his companion in a spirit of helpfulness, "You step in front of de white man." Shocked that the Kittitian's friend was referring to *him*, the African American, who had grown up under racial segregation in the American Deep South and saw himself as something of a pan-Africanist, became unaccountably angry and spoke sharply to the young man, who had meant no harm. "I'm not a white man. Don't call me a white man." This elicited from the two Kittitians looks of bemusement.

Not long after this incident, a local "black" man with light skin, who was well-to-do and widely traveled, said wryly to me, "In St. Kitts, I am white. In England, I am colored. In America, I am black."

Publicly acknowledged or not, much of the Haitian elite's organic antipathy toward their black president could be ascribed to race and color as well as class antagonism, this last bit of bad energy activated the first time the president began taking steps toward social policies designed to benefit the country's black poor.

Only upon visiting Haiti does the place strike one as remarkably reminiscent of the old racialist South Africa.* Had this situation been more widely noticed by the outside world, perhaps the white and mulatto elites might have been pressured onto a course of constructive compromise while a vestige of the new democracy remained to be salvaged. As it was, they continued to behave like the eagerly overindulged insular people that they were, some even venturing far

---

* C. L. R. James commented about the similarities in 1980, forty-two years after the publication of his landmark book on the Haitian revolution: "A copy of it (*The Black Jacobins*) was in the library in South Africa, though they (the blacks students) didn't know anything about it, until a white professor there told them: 'I suggest you read *The Black Jacobins* in the library; you may find it useful.' Eagerly they got the book, read it and found it a revelation, particularly in the relations between black South Africans and Coloreds who are people of mixed race, black and white. They typed out copies, mimeographed them and circulated passages from *The Black Jacobins* dealing with relations between the blacks and the mixed in Haiti. I could not help thinking that revolution moves in mysterious ways, its wonders to perform."

enough into the regions of bad taste as to place grotesquely racist caricatures of the president on their websites. Unlike neighboring Caribbean islands where black and white children may be found learning together in the same classroom, such scenes are all but impossible to find in Haiti, arguably the Caribbean's most racially segregated and class-riven society.

Even elements of the international community who defend the unseemly excesses of Haiti's wealthy were often shocked by the breadth of the divide that separates Haiti's rich from its poor.

In January 2003, Denis Paradis, Canada's powerful secretary of state, went so far as to convene a secret meeting in Ottawa to draw up plans to overthrow the Aristide government before the January 1, 2004, bicentennial celebration. The blueprint for the planned coup was known as the Ottawa Initiative on Haiti.

But even Paradis, coming from one of the wealthiest nations on earth, was dumbstruck on first witnessing the wealth of Haiti's apartheid-reminiscent upper class: "The rich are so rich there," he said. "I've visited a few rich places there, the rich are so rich, I'd never seen anything like that . . . but the poor is unbelievable [sic]."

10

Port-au-Prince, Haiti
Tuesday, December 17, 2002, 3:00 A.M.

IT HAD BEEN AN UNEVENTFUL SUNDAY EVENING.
Save for distant birdsong and the keen chirp of crickets, the night space was windless and quiet. At three in the morning, the Champs de Mars, which runs across the frontage of the National Palace grounds, was void of motor and foot traffic.

A handful of CAT team members patrolled in the shadows behind the heavy wrought iron fence circumscribing the palace area. The white, exquisitely designed building caught the moonlight, which imparted a property of incandescence to the neoclassical masterpiece. The building housed the offices of the president, Jean-Bertrand Aristide, and the members of his cabinet. It also included an apartment in which the president, his wife, Mildred, and two young daughters, Christine and Michaëlle, resided from Monday to

Friday afternoon before leaving for their own home in Tabarre on weekends.

The CAT team officers strolling the grounds wore bulletproof vests over khaki shirts with dark blue pants. They carried no radios. They were armed with forty-year-old M1 rifles and a few rounds of ammo of equivalent age. In training, the officers were allotted six rounds to qualify on the decrepit, unreliable weapons. For backup, the CAT team officers had two vintage M60s with pitted barrels salvaged from the weapons depot of the old demobilized Duvalierist army.

Two of the officers near the ornate palace gate on the Champs de Mars heard the scream of revving engines and burning tires just as a line of heavy-duty trucks, retrofitted with track-mounted M50 machine guns, rumbled across the boulevard and smashed through the iron leaves of the tall gate. The two officers were killed where they stood by rebels firing M16s from the beds of the lead trucks. The rebels then raked the walls of the palace with six-inch-long rounds fired from the deafening M50 machine guns. The earsplitting noise, sounding like a rapid succession of sharp thunderclaps, was unlike anything the palace police had ever heard before. They would later recall that the walls of the palace shook when penetrated by the big rounds that were twice the size of those fired from the officers' own unreliable M60s.

The battle was over before it began. The rebels entered the palace and set about vandalizing the interior. Their leader, the former Delmas district police captain Guy Philippe, announced via closed circuit from the palace communications center to the Port-au-Prince police commanders, who were equipped with radios, that his forces had taken the palace and he was in charge of the country.

Learning what had happened, angry residents of the capital milled onto the plaza, in effect surrounding the rebels who had available to them only the supplies they brought with them in their trucks.

Either the rebels were performing an act of lethal theater on orders from offstage controllers, or they had badly miscalculated the public reaction to the raid on the palace. While it is not known what the rebels may have expected to achieve, they could hardly have expected a warm reception from the police and the residents of Port-au-Prince.

The rebels, unlike the police, had the wherewithal to communicate instantly by radio telephone with foreign and local officials in Santo Dominigo, hundreds of miles away. The rebels' radio signals were bounced along repeaters or relays that had been installed on the highest peaks between Port-au-Prince and the capital of the Dominican Republic. Unsurprisingly, the coup attempt (if that is what the raid was) collapsed and the heavily armed rebels, appearing at a loss for further tactical ideas, reboarded their trucks and sped through the night toward their camp across the border in the Dominican Republic.

At the time, the raid was generally considered another in a series of botched coup attempts undertaken by brazen rebels who made no effort to hide their identity. In retrospect, however, the events of that Sunday evening were likely not the failure they first appeared to be. Given what was to happen on February 29, 2004, and *how* it happened, what the rebels did (whether they themselves knew it or not) was part of a larger strategy to create in Haiti, episode by violent episode, a general impression of escalating instability that could be ascribed to a homegrown group of people. The well-armed thugs, who doubtless envisioned themselves as supplanting the president in power, were discardable pawns in a larger diversion, planned and implemented by others.

The afternoon following the attack, the president went to the National Palace and made a speech to reassure the country. On the ground near a tree not far from where the president had spoken rested a wooden ammo box left behind by the rebels the night before. Stenciled on the long sides of the box were the words *United States Army*.

11

Port-au-Prince, Haiti
Friday, February 7, 2003

ON FEBRUARY 7, 2003, THE PRESIDENT
raised the country's national minimum wage from thirty-five
gourds to seventy gourds (US$2) a day.

The initiative touched off a firestorm of protest. One of the most
vigorous expressions of opposition came over the public airways
from Andy Apaid, a Syrian American who operated several large
sweatshops in Haiti, including the Apaid Garment Factory, a large
scant-wage apparel manufacturing facility on Toussaint L'Ouverture
Boulevard in Port-au-Prince. Apaid, who was born in New York and
was not a Haitian citizen, also served as a leader of Group 184, a
wealthy antidemocratic groupuscule that had been demanding the
president's resignation and exit, as if two decisive and undisputed nationwide presidential elections had not occurred.

Speakers could be heard amplifying his sentiments on Radio Metropole, a powerful, privately owned radio station broadcasting mostly in French to listeners outside the country, not Kreyol-speaking Haitians. Radio Metropole, a founding member of Group 184, criticized virtually every social policy the democratic government promulgated, including the new minimum wage measure. Inasmuch as the vast majority of Haiti's radio stations were owned by the wealthy class, the reform-minded but overmatched president could not hope to win a contest of radio signals. Of course the antigovernment stations never covered successful government projects, ranging from hospital to public school openings, which in the latter case ran into the hundreds.

While the Haitian people supported the president they had twice elected by huge margins, the Haitian upper class and the regenerative black remnants of the old Duvalierist military dictatorship were implacably opposed to him and to the essential democratic idea of his government.

The president was an idealist in the mold of the republic's founder, Toussaint L'Ouverture, who fought and defeated armies from Spain, England, and France in a partly successful effort to win for black Haitians elemental human freedom as well as economic and social equality. The resurgent Duvalierists, who had traditionally provided the black iron veil of brute force and public color to wealthy whites and mulattoes, were no more interested in universal freedom for their fellow black Haitians than were the racist elites with whom they were symbiotically engaged.

Before the president's election, Haiti, on an operational level, could be likened to racialist South Africa. In exchange for the trappings of state power, the dictator Francois Duvalier and his black successors gave to the white and mulatto upper class a free hand to exploit the huge black, largely illiterate labor force in any way it saw fit. Black despots were indulged with the summary power of life and death over the poor black majority. In exchange, the white and mulatto business class was allowed a camouflaged hiding place with carte blanche to create for itself a cash flow virtually undiminished by wage or tax or ordinary utilities remittances.

This was the Faustian bargain that Aristide threatened with his stunning first election victory of December 16, 1990. His mandate, as he saw it, was to change Haiti fundamentally. For it, he had only the structureless popular support of the newly enfranchised poor black masses that had bought him to power.

Uncomfortable with what the president's vision for Haiti could mean for their interests, both private and public, the United States and France, from the beginning, took up positions on the opposite side of the ideological divide, putting themselves in the working company of a tiny, ruthlessly antidemocratic minority.

●　　●　　●

An American friend, an academic of considerable reputation, telephoned about a year ago and said, "I am sending you something I think you'll find interesting."

"What's it about?" I asked.

"Look, just read it."

"Sure. Fine."

Within minutes I had received a twenty-three-page, single-spaced fax. Though I was already late for an appointment, I sat down to read, skipping about a bit.

. . . it is a remarkable and lamentable fact, that while Haiti. . . is trying to be a sister republic and anxious to have a government of the people. . . she is the one country to which we turn the cold shoulder.

Mole St. Nicolas (in Haiti) is a splendid harbor. It is properly styled the Gibraltar of the country. It commands the Windward Passage, (shipping lane between Cuba and Haiti), the natural gateway of the commerce. . . . we (the United States) want this harbor for a naval station. It is seen that the nation that can get it and hold it will be master of the land and sea in its neighborhood. Some rash things have been said by Americans about getting possession of this harbor. We are to have it peaceably, if we can, forcibly, if we must.

. . . In the towns and cities of the country, the people are largely of mixed blood and range all the way from black to white. But the people of the interior are of pure (African) blood. The prevailing color among them is a dark brown. . . . They are in many respects a fine looking people. There is about them a sort of majesty. They carry themselves proudly erect as if conscious of their freedom and independence. . . .

The common people of Haiti are peaceful enough. They have no taste for revolutions. The fault is not with the. . . many, but with the educated and ambitious few. . . . Governed neither by love nor mercy for their country, they care not into what depths she may be plunged. No president, however, virtuous, wise and patriotic, ever suits them when they themselves happen to be out of power.

I wish I could say that these are the only conspirators against the peace of Haiti, but I cannot. They have allies in the United States. . . . It so happens that we have men in this country (the United States) who, to accomplish their personal and selfish ends, will fan the flames of passion between the factions in Haiti and will otherwise assist in setting revolutions afoot. To this shame. . . men in high American quarters have boasted to me of their ability to start a revolution in Haiti at pleasure. They have only to raise sufficient money, they say, with which to arm and otherwise equip the malcontents. . . to effect their object. . . . To them, the welfare of Haiti is nothing; the shedding of human blood is nothing; the success of free institutions is nothing and the ruin of neighboring country is nothing. . . .

You will ask me about the President of Haiti. I will tell you. Whatever may be said or thought of him to the contrary, I affirm that there is no man in Haiti who more fully understands or more deeply feels the need of peace in his country.

. . . (and) instead of receiving the sympathy and support of the American Press and people, this man has been denounced as a cruel monster. I declare to you, than this, no judgement of President Hyppolite could be more unjust and more undeserved."

I stopped.

President *Hyppolite?*

I then turned to the last page and saw along the bottom:

Lecture *on* Haiti

The Haitian Pavillion
Dedication Ceremonies Delivered at the World's Fair
Jackson Park, Chicago
January 2, 1893
By the Honorable Frederick Douglass
Ex-Minister to Haiti

12

Washington, D.C.
2003

OVER THE COURSE OF 2003, THE BUSH administration broadened its assault on Haiti into a crippling, multipronged campaign. In addition to arming the Duvalierist insurgents and organizing Haiti's tiny, splintered political opposition, the administration moved apace to strangle Haiti, the poorest country in the Western Hemisphere, into a state of economic, social, and political collapse.

The fix was in: The U.S. Agency for International Development and the International Republican Institute (the international arm of the Republican Party) had spent tens of millions of dollars to create and organize an opposition—however small in numbers—and to make Haiti under Aristide ungovernable. The whole scenario was strikingly similar to the series of events that led to the coup against Venezuelan President Hugo Chávez in April 2002. The same U.S. organizations were involved, and the opposition—as in Venezuela—controlled and used the major media as a tool for destabilization. And in both cases, the coup leaders, joined by Washington, announced to the world that the elected president had "voluntarily re-signed"—which later turned out to be false.

Washington had an added weapon against the Haitian government. Taking advantage of Haiti's desperate poverty and dependence on foreign aid, it stopped international aid to the government, from the summer of 2000 until the 2004 coup. As economist Jeffrey Sachs has pointed out, the World Bank also contributed to the destabilization ef-fort by cutting off funding.

MARK WEISBROT
The Nation

Taking pains to close off every possible economic escape route to the government of Haiti, the Bush administration took measures of dubious legality to block four loans of $146 million that had been fully approved by the Inter-American Development Bank (IDB) in 1998. The loans were targeted for projects that would benefit the poor of Haiti in four critical areas—clean drinking water, health, ed-ucation, and roads. In anticipation of the loan proceeds, the Haitian government had been forced by the IDB, at the instigation of the United States, to pay $5 million interest for loan money that the Haitian government would never see a penny of.

In response to Washington's suffocating obstructionism, the Robert F. Kennedy Memorial Foundation brought suit in the U.S. Federal District Court in Washington, D.C., against the IDB over its Haiti policy. Todd Howland, the executive director of the foundation, explained:

> On the IDB's website, there are glowing reports about the outstanding work that the IDB is doing in Haiti. What they do not mention is that the IDB never actually funded these projects. . . as a result, Haitians have died. There have been actual deaths linked to the fact that the IDB never disbursed these loans. . .
>
> We are taking action in tort and in contract. The government of Haiti acted on behalf of third-party beneficiaries—the people of Haiti. The government signed and ratified loans and also *paid* five millions dollars to the IDB in anticipation of recovering the benefits of this contract. Haiti received nothing.

Although the Bush administration had employed meanness against any number of small, poor countries that had inadvertently run afoul of Washington, its treatment of Haiti was out of the ordinary. Quite gratuitously, the United States seemed to have done everything possible, save unleashing a full-bore air bombardment of Port-au-Prince, to maximize the suffering of a people, who, for the first time in two hundred years, were living under a government of their own clear choice.

No one could think of an occasion when the United States had gone so far out of its way to spoil for a small, defenseless republic the simple observance of its own national birthday, particularly when the country was not its enemy. It was madness—a vengeful, scripted, slow-burn madness that had run unbroken for two hundred years.

13

Paris, France
December 2003

O N April 7, 2003, the bicentennial of
Toussaint L'Overture's death, President Aristide announced
the findings of a restitution commission formed by his government.
The commission determined that France owed Haiti $21 billion, the
value in current dollars of the money France extorted from Haiti following its successful slave rebellion. On October 12, 2003, the president convened a four-day international conference of experts at
Haiti's National Palace to further discuss Haiti's resitution claim
against France for repayment of the debt. Among the participants
were French historian, human rights commissioner, and author of
The Crime of Napoleon, Claube Ribbe, and Tulane law school professor Günther Handl, a responsed authority on international law.

Indeed, much of Haiti's current problems are directly at-
tributable to the exploitation and repression during
France's colonial rule, as well as the brutal, far-reaching
measures imposed on Haiti by the major powers in response to Haiti's declaration of independence... Argu-
ments supporting France's right to have drained Haiti's
treasury were not persuasive 200 years ago, and they are
not persuasive now. As legal scholars and litigants, we are
willing to work with Haiti to seek redress from France, and
this deserves broad-based international support.

> PROFESSOR CHARLES OGLETREE
> *Harvard Law School*

France was not the only Western society that would capitalize an
industrial economy with proceeds amassed from slave labor. The
United States, Spain, Holland, Denmark, and Great Britain would
do much the same.

The personal and public wealth of Britain created by slave
labour was a crucial element in the accumulation of capital
that made the industrial revolution possible, and the sur-
viving profits have remained a sold element with specific
families and within British society generally, cascading
down from generation to generation, in John Major's felici-
tous phrase. In this context, the demand for reparations is
a serious position, similar to the claim put forward by the
nations of Holocaust survivors for the return of property
stolen by the Nazis. Black people whose forebears were

slaves, victims of that other Holocaust, are simply asking
for the stolen fruits of their ancestors' labour power to be
given back to their rightful heirs.

RICHARD GOTT
Guardian
January 17, 2007

If Britain owes reparations to the descendants of the enslaved
Africans whose uncompensated labor, in large part, financed Britain's
industrial revolution, France owes Haiti a great deal more than the
$21 billion Haiti applied for in late 2003.

Over a century and a half, France not only appropriated the worth of
Haiti's enslaved population's toil but also forced Haiti to pay reparations to France following the Haitian revolution. France's real debt to
Haiti thus amounts to the $21 billion France exacted, in addition to the
assessed value of the labor of the Africans France enslaved in Haiti from
the mid-seventeenth century to the end of the slave revolt in 1804.

One month after the conference, in December 2003, French foreign minister Dominique de Villepin sent his sister to Port-au-
Prince to tell Jean-Bertrand Aristide, the democratically elected
president, that it was time for him to step down.

Aristide had been sworn into office in 1991 with the modest and
reasonable hope of improving the lot of the Haitian poor by the
smallest of increments. He went to lengths to warn down the expec-
tations of his exuberant supporters who had voted for the first time
in their lives. In speeches and formal papers, the president told the
nation that his overall objective was twofold. First, he would seek to
ameliorate the long-standing poverty of millions by requiring a more

equitable balance of load bearing between the very rich and the very poor. In the president's own cautionary words, he would try his best to lift the poorest of the poor "from misery to poverty with dignity." For the first time the rich would be asked to pay significant taxes, as well as for electricity and telephone services they received. For workers, the president would seek something more than their pittance of a wage, which was lower than the smallest sums paid to workers elsewhere in the region, if not the lowest in the world.

The president's second major objective was to make democracy, which was new to his country, into a habit that would strengthen as practice was followed by more practice. Over and over, he announced in one speech after another, "We must learn in our country to move from election to election." This was how democracy for Haiti was to be learned, how its governments were to be changed, how its transitions were to be ritualized. The president knew that the requisite patience and forbearance would not be easy in a country that had no real experience with democracy and had suffered through thirty-four coups d'état in its history, most of them inspired by outside forces.

Given the powerful influence of the president's enemies, both inside and outside the country, the two broad objectives he set out proved to be irreconcilable. Had the president's advocacy on behalf of the poor not annoyed members of the business class, the modern mulatto class (along with its powerful American and French backers) he might have been allowed the ceremonial, albeit empty victory of going from "election to election."

As it was, the great powers, led by the United States, made clear to the antigovernment kvetchers they coached and funded inside Haiti that the fate of the president had never been in the president's hands, or, for that matter, in the hands of the Haitian electorate.

What was it, though, about Haiti that made the place so different from other Caribbean places, so especially combustible? What property, what special character did it have that would incite the rich white West to engage a poor, largely black nation with such glowering, unrelenting hostility?

Most, who have been brought up in the West, have been socialized to define the term *poverty* too narrowly—to fathom the condition's material face alone and to the exclusion of all else, as if there were no more pernicious and debilitating forms of the condition than one might perceive with the naked eye.

At a polling station in the northern countryside, I once looked at a line of Haitian voters and measured them by their dress and bearing to be poor. In making this assessment, I hadn't needed to look beyond what I could *see*. This was how I had been trained, or rather mistrained, throughout my life—to look shallowly at a human being as one would the surface of an object, seeing nothing more than the little the eye can take in.

But what can a cloth suit tell me about the wealth of a soul?

After all, the "poorest" Haitian peasant knew his or her *story* in a way that I had never known mine. This may have been because I had forgotten mine, or was it because I had never been told it? Other formerly colonized Caribbeans, seemed to be in much the same boat as I.

The Haitians *knew* their history. The Haitian peasants may have had few material possessions to speak of, but they knew what their slave ancestors had done to the French, to the English and to the Spanish. They also knew what they had done to liberate all of Latin America, as well as themselves. No matter how poor they were, the Haitians knew these things about themselves, things that made them special to themselves, that made them resilient and independent, that gave them great *art*, that unsettled, even now, those nations the peasants' slave ancestors had once soundly thrashed.

In the last analysis, the knowledge of one's own foundation story may be the most consoling, indeed, the most empowering form of wealth there is—a wealth more sustaining over time than all the worldly goods one could conceive of.

Preparing in 1953 to attack the Moncada barracks to start the Cuban revolution with a handful of men, Fidel Castro and his followers read over and again the story of how the great black Cuban general, Antonio Maceo, had championed Cuba's war of liberation against Spain.

Castro later wrote of his fighters' studies in a letter:

> Homer's *Iliad* contains no events more heroic, and our *Mambis* (Cuban independence fighters in the war against Spain) seem more legendary than they, Achilles less invincible than Maceo. Why must we live in ignorance of our great feat. . . . If children were to grow up exposed to such examples and inspired by those great souls, who could ever subjugate them?

Haiti had likely erected more statues to honor the memory of its heroes than had all the rest of the Caribbean community combined. Indeed, the impulse to do such things troubled the Haitian wealthy class considerably. While knowledge, in and of itself, was a form of wealth, it was also a powerful weapon.

During the run-up to the events of February 2004, the American-armed paramilitaries, upon arriving in Gonaïves, tore down the statue of Alexandre Pétion, one of the country's most broadly revered presidents.*

When the thugs who'd been collaborating with Haiti's wealthy class finally entered Port-au-Prince in the days following the president's mysterious disappearance, they destroyed first off the Museum of the Restitution.†

---

* Alexandre Sabés Pétion (1770–1818), president of Haiti from 1806 to 1818, like Toussaint L'Ouverture and Jean-Jacques Dessalines before him, supported the idea of ridding the world of slavery. In exchange for a commitment to abolish slavery in Latin America, Pétion provided Simón Bolívar, the South American revolutionary, with sanctuary, money, arms, and a printing press with which to successfully wage his war against Spain that produced independence for five Latin American states.

† The Museum of the Restitution, housed in the former army headquarters, assembled hundreds of entries (paintings, sculptures) produced of a nationwide arts contest on themes of the bicentennial, the restitution, liberty, justice, and so on.

14

National Palace grounds, Port-au-Prince, Haiti
Thursday, January 1, 2004, 8:00 A.M.

FOREIGN MINISTER NKOSAZANA DLAMINI Zuma traveled halfway around the world with her president, Thabo Mbeki, to attend Haiti's bicentennial celebration on January 1.

She remarked to Hazel, my wife, that "Haiti's revolution was too magnificent an accomplishment for all blacks everywhere, for South Africa not to be in Haiti today."

Hazel described the occasion in an entry to her journal:

> The morning breeze was cool and fresh as I stepped out of my hotel and onto the paved courtyard.
>
> It was January 1, 2004—exactly two hundred years to the day since Jean-Jacques Dessalines and hundreds of thousands of former slaves stood in Gonaïves, victorious

after a grueling thirteen-year war, and declared France's former slave colony of St. Domingue the independent Republic of Haiti.

I was humbled and deeply moved to be on this hallowed ground on this sacred day, where so many blacks had fought and died and bled and triumphed.

Lush tropical foliage—poincianas, palm trees, dramatic vines, and plants with bold splashes of color, posed brightly as Haiti's visitors readied themselves—getting into cars, waiting for colleagues, asking last-minute questions of hotel staff, being helped by the pleasant protocol officers provided by the government—to head to the National Palace for the official ceremony.

To get to the palace, we had to turn off the hotel road and on to, fittingly, John Brown Avenue—named after the fearless American abolitionist who had been profoundly inspired by the Haitian revolution, and had led an armed uprising at Harpers Ferry, West Virginia, to end slavery in the United States. When the U.S. Government hanged Brown, flags all across Haiti were flown at half-mast. John Brown's raid on behalf of millions of blacks enslaved in America unleashed tensions and hatreds in the United States that contributed to the start of the Civil War and the eventual abolition of slavery in America.

Haiti's original Amerindian inhabitants had named their land Ayiti—Land of Many Mountains. And it is easy to understand why. The drive from Pétion-Ville, where many hotels are located, to downtown Port-au-Prince takes you along the inside curve of full, round hills that dip seductively into a deep and beguiling declivity before rising again on the other side.

The streets still had that early morning feel as we drove down the hillside and towards the city and the palace— there were some people walking briskly in this direction, while others strode the other way. But there was nothing either in the expressions of the people, or of their numbers to indicate that this was either New Years Day or Haiti's Bicentennial.

As we approached Champs de Mars, (the area of wide boulevards and large parks before one actually gets to the palace) I saw people drifting toward the general area of the palace. I noticed that bleachers had been set up immediately in front of and across the street from the palace. . . . I took my seat on a raised platform in front of the palace, facing the street and the bleachers and watched with a sense of wonderment as the ocean of black, proud humanity continued to swell. Arisitide began to speak, and the crowds roared. He spoke some more and soon the crowd was singing cherished Haitian melodies in the morning sunshine. Proud and joyous Haitians stretched as far as the eye could see. After a while, however, the pressure of the people against the palace's wrought iron fence became so great that a part of both the wrought iron and the concrete wall gave way. The people welcomed this opportunity and started flowing onto the palace grounds in calm, triumphant waves despite the many security guards standing inside the fence. Aristide continued speaking, calmly, never missing a beat, as the sea of humanity kept moving towards the palace and the special guests seated on the platform. The Haitians sitting on the dais continued listening and alternately applauding and smiling, while thousands upon thousands of Haitians on the lawn kept moving towards us. Ambassador Luigi Einaudi, the Organization of American States (OAS) official with ultimate authority for Haiti policy was seated next to me on the dais. He began whispering to me in an air of clear, if controlled, panic "They're going to riot . . . they're going to riot."

But they did not.

They came toward the dais up until that point where lawn gave way to the driveway, and there they stopped. They listened, they clapped, they cheered, they joyously thrust all five fingers into the air to signal to the world that the days of coups were over, and that Aristide, as Haiti's elected president, would serve the five years of his term. The huge palace lawn was now packed solid, yet outside the gates people still stretched toward the horizon.

Einuadi was the son of an Italian President and the OAS' most senior official on Haiti policy. His principal responsibility was to broker an agreement between Aristide and Haiti's unelected "opposition," Convergence, a responsibility he made little or no attempt to discharge.

I leaned over and said to him: "Look at this outpouring of love and support for the President. No one can say he does not have the support of the people." Einaudi said, "Well, he does not have the support of the real people. It is just these types of people here who support him" (pointing dismissively to the hundreds of thousands massed before him).

I then asked him: "What percentage of the population do these people represent?" He answered, "Well eighty to ninety percent, but they're not the ones who matter."

Shortly after arriving earlier that morning at Haiti's National Palace, Hazel spotted U.S. Representative Maxine Waters and her husband, Ambassador Sidney Williams, standing at the top of the stone palace steps. As they embraced, Waters whispered to Hazel, "They're planning a coup you know. They're planning a coup. I've been going to receptions at various hotels over the past few days.

"They've been held by business types and the *convergence* types and that is all the talk. They tried to get me not to come—the State Department. CBC [Congressional Black Caucus] members were planning to be here and State called them and told them that it was too dangerous. That they couldn't ensure their safety. That's why the caucus delegation canceled. The State Department put a warning on their website telling people not to come to Haiti now. They tried that with me. I told them that I was coming. No matter what, I was coming."

15

L ITTLE HAD CHANGED IN TWO HUNDRED YEARS.
Representative Waters, her husband, Ambassador Sidney
Williams, President Thabo Mbeki, my wife, Hazel, President
Aristide, his democratic government, and millions of Haitians
were celebrating the free black republic that Jean-Jacques
Dessalines and his fighters proudly established in 1804. Yet the
U.S. State Department was readying to fulfill the angry pledge of
Thomas Jefferson's son-in-law, Senator Eppes of Virginia, "to ven-
ture the treasury of the United States that the Negro government
should be destroyed."

It was almost as if the United States did not want to let another revolution in the New World rank with its own, yet
Haiti's was in many ways a more "impossible" and thor-
ough overthrow of a European regime, and it had more

immediate imitators in this hemisphere than did the
"Spirit of 1776."

Garry Wills
The Negro President

Where the poor were concerned, the United States invariably opposed the efforts of the poor's own governments, whenever and
wherever those governments tried in any serious or structured way to
ameliorate the poverty of their own people. If there has ever been a
circumstance in which the Americans did not take the side of the
rich in efforts to quash even modest reforms to help the poor, I do
not know of it.

In Haiti's case, the United States, directly or indirectly through its
Haitian collaborators, blocked every path the poor, through their
elected leaders, took to win for themselves a less painful existence.
And, following the antidemocratic and antipoor violence of its collaborators, the Camericans, it warned the world away from a Haitian
bicentennial celebration that it had calculatedly endeavored to ruin.*

Throughout 2003, blacks around the world labored to make
Haiti's bicentennial celebration an event of global significance. In
America, radio stations had begun taping public service announce-
ments made by Bill and Camille Cosby, Frederick Douglass IV, Alvin
Poussaint, Ossie Davis and Ruby Dee, Kenyan and Jamaican schol-
ars, Ali Mazrui, and Rex Nettleford, legendary calypsonian Mighty
Sparrow. For example:

---

* *Camericans* is a name for citizens and residents of Caribbean countries who by
their actions demonstrate a higher loyalty to America and its purposes than they
do to their own countries and people.

This is Bill Cosby

All my life I've been fascinated by the Haitian revolution. Toussaint L'Ouverture, Christophe, Dessalines, and the hundreds of thousands of slave revolutionaries who rose up and defeated the mightiest armies of Europe are very much alive in my heart.

However, the Haitian people not only freed themselves, they proclaimed Haiti a refuge for escaped slaves from *anywhere* in the world.

Thank-you, Haiti.

Haiti shook the foundations of slavery *everywhere* in 1804. Throughout all of 2004, we will remember.

Celebrate the Haitian revolution.

Fought by Haitians.

Won for us all.

On American university campuses, including Harvard, Brown, and Columbia, conferences and colloquia had been planned for 2004 marking the triumph of Haitian slaves two hundred years before.

A charter flight of American artists, writers, elected officials, and leaders was to have been laid on for the January 1 event in Port-au-Prince, which would open a year of worldwide commemorative programs.

Washington responded by stoking violence which it then used to label Haiti and its bicentennial celebration unsafe for American visitors and foreign visitors in general. Owing to the growing U.S.-inspired instability, American newspapers, virtually en masse, took up the story line that "Haiti had nothing to celebrate." In fact, however, Haiti was under attack, as always, precisely because it had so much to celebrate—an extraordinary foundation story to bolster the spirits of contemporary Haitians as well as blacks globally—a germinal event of spectacular valor and attainment that, sadly, remained every bit as galling to Washington and Paris in 2004 as it had been to Jefferson and Bonaparte in 1804.

16

Washington, D.C.
Wednesday, February 25, 2004

O N FEBRUARY 25, 2004, ANGRY MEMBERS of the Congressional Black Caucus marched to the White House without an appointment and demanded a meeting with President George W. Bush. They were told by the national security adviser, Condoleezza Rice, that the president was not available, whereupon the bestirred black representatives promised that they would hold an impromptu press conference on the looming Haitian emergency in front of the White House. Hearing this, Rice expressed a newfound confidence that she could indeed pry the president out of his "meeting."

The president met with the delegation and somehow mollified it into an unfortunate state of public silence. Delusionally triumphant, the black representatives left the White House, declining to go on record to the press and the world with a strong position on the rapidly deteriorating situation in Haiti.

It is not known, *nor does it matter*, what the president said about the Haitian crisis in his off-the-record meeting with the members of the Congressional Black Caucus that day. What *did* matter was what the president declined to say publicly or via back channel to the rebels who were well along at that point toward shattering Haiti's fragile democracy. Had the president of the United States ordered the rebels to stand down, there can be little doubt that Guy Philippe and his men would have complied instantly. But the president did not do this, either privately or publicly. It would be weeks before the reasons for this could be learned.

Tabarre, Haiti
Saturday, February 28, 2004, 11:35 P.M. EST

THE TELEPHONE IN THE PRESIDENT'S RESI-
dence at Tabarre rang twice before sending a sharp click
through the cranky connection. A long buzzing noise ended in a
male voice that sounded watery and faraway.

"Yes."

The American voice did not belong to the house.

"Good evening. This is Randall Robinson for President Aristide."

A short silence. Dead space.

"He is not here."

I waited, but the voice had finished its business.

"Can you tell me when he will be back?"

Again, the empty silence.

"No." Louder this time.

"May I speak with Madame Aristide?"

"She is not here."

The voice had become less neutral.

"Can you tell me when she will be returning?"

"No."

"When Madame Aristide returns, would you tell her. . ."

The line had gone dead.

Watching me, Hazel asked, "What is it?"

"I'm not sure."

●   ●   ●

Some years earlier, I had gone to Haiti to serve as a monitor for the country's parliamentary elections. I was part of a team that covered a small number of polling stations in the deep rural north of the country. Democracy was still a new idea in the country. The black poor were to take a seat at the country's decisionmaking table for the first time in Haiti's troubled two-hundred-year history.

The first polling station on our list, an ancient one-room wooden affair, had not yet opened when our group of four black Americans approached in a leased minivan. We chugged around a blind bend in the winding dirt road and glimpsed a file of people who were quietly waiting in the searing hot morning sun. The line snaked forward along the dusty road for the better part of a mile, or so it seemed to me. I remember that the people were standing very close to each other, their backs starched in a conspicuously formal posture. They gave the impression of sheltering one another from some unknown and nonspecific consequence they feared would befall them as a price for their democratic daring. They were old and young. They were dressed as though they had come to the polling station from church, the men in their threadbare suits, the women looking remarkably African in the bright primary colors of their wraps. It was not Sunday, however, but a weekday, around nine in the morning.

Rounding the curve and into view, there seemed something almost worth crying about in the sheer beauty of the vista—something so compellingly unforgettable in the pride and purpose written on the faces of these wretchedly poor people who were on that very morning, and in the remotest of places, coming, at long last, into ownership of their own country.

We stayed there until the last person in line, an elderly man, had voted. He was seventy-seven years old and illiterate. He possessed nothing except the modest house his family lived in, the faded, ill-fitting suit he wore for the morning's great occasion, and his everyday work clothes.

I asked him his name through a translator.

"My name is Pierre Aristide."

I did not know at the time that *Aristide* is not an uncommon name in the country. Seeing the question in my eyes, he said, "No, I am not family to the president but," he touched his breast, "in here I am," and smiled.

I had only been in the country for a day or so and had little opportunity to learn much. Driving in the countryside, however, I came to appreciate emotionally for the first time how widespread and painful Haiti's poverty is, and that the *color* of that poverty was all but exclusively black.

I asked the old man what he meant.

"The president is our hope," he answered. "He and we are the same." When I seemed to require more, he said, "Not just here on the outside," touching the dark skin on his arm, "but here on the inside," his hand again placed over his heart.

"First time for us." Then almost wistfully, his old eyes welling, "First time for us."

He told me in so many words that he had come there that day to do his little part to help the president who was the first "important man" in all his long years who had wanted to help him and others like him who were black and poor.

He was sitting on a low stone wall at the time looking down at the hard black ground when he told me these things. I waited for him to continue while he decided whether he wished to or not.

"I don't think Haiti is like other countries [pronouncing the name *Ayiti*]. Here, the rich people don't want the black people to have *anything*."

He seemed to forget about the translator's presence and lifted his clouded, rheumy eyes to mine.

"Nothing! Nothing!" The words were said with a conviction I'd thought beyond the old man's physical reserves.

"He's going to have a hard time. Our president is going to have a hard time. I pray for him everyday. I pray for him everyday."

The old man owned virtually nothing—not even his own pain, it would seem—for those who had been responsible for that pain furiously denied what, if anything, was owed to him for that, and before too long, had so burdened the public's understanding with deflection and noise, as to deny the old man's very existence in every place but in the sight of God.

●　●　●

In the weeks leading up to the tumult of February 29, 2004, the president and his wife carried on as usual. The threats to the government were real enough. The president had abided them, since his second term began on February 7, 2001, as the unavoidable price of effecting reform in a country that had always been irreconcilably divided between the very rich, the not so very rich, and the very poor, or, more tellingly, between whites, mulattoes, and opportunist black rulers on the one hand, and the wretchedly deprived "peasants" on the other. They were nearly all black and comprised the vast majority of the country's 8 million people. It was from their ranks that the president rose in 1990 from a field of thirteen candidates to win the country's first free and fair presidential election by taking 67 percent of the vote. He was a Roman Catholic priest back then, and took seriously the vow he made to the poor of working to ease their misery.

The challenge he embraced would prove more difficult than he or others in the popular movement at first imagined.

18

Port-au-Prince, Haiti
Saturday, February 28, 2004

ABANDONED BY THE WORLD'S LEADING DEMOC-
racies as thugs roamed the countryside, emptied jails, and
burned police stations, ordinary Haitians by the thousands dragged
out large objects—containers, rusted-out trucks, boulders, discarded
refrigerators, rubber tires—and mounded them into a protective cor-
don around the National Palace and across key thoroughfares leading into Port-au-Prince.

U.S. officials called for calm and promised to make the rebels
come to the negotiation table with the democratic government. They
then asked President Aristide to have his civilian defenders stand
down and remove the makeshift barriers in the interest of peace. It
was at this turn that Secretary of State Powell made the homiletic re-
mark that the U.S. government would not allow "thugs" to remove a
democratically elected government. The secretary (whose statement

would only technically prove to be true, depending on one's definition of *thugs*) apparently intended to convince Aristide that the United States was prepared to deal firmly with the rebels, so that Aristide would open the city by removing the barricades. Prepared to talk, Aristide appealed to his supporters to dismantle the barriers. As soon as the streets had been cleared, however, the rebels, Andy Apaid, and the leaders of Group 184 refused to discuss anything other than the president's unconditional departure from Haiti.

Around the same time, the international media began showing American soldiers landing in Haiti "to protect the embassy and American lives."

During the day of Saturday, February 28, the city remained open and undefended, its arteries all but free of obstruction. The rebels roamed far to the north of Port-au-Prince, somewhere between Gonaïves and Cap-Haitien. The president was at home at Tabarre with Mrs. Aristide preparing for Sunday interviews at the National Palace with Tavis Smiley and George Stephanopoulous. A few miles away, a few dozen lightly armed police patrolled the National Palace grounds.

In the country "to provide security for their embassies and citizens," the only soldiers of any kind present that day in Port-au-Prince were American, French, and Canadian forces. Their numbers were unknown to the government of Haiti.

19

THE TELEPHONE RANG IN OUR HOME SHORTLY
after the last of the three failed attempts I made that evening
to get through to President and Mrs. Aristide. Hazel answered. It was
Tavis Smiley of National Public Radio. Hazel worked with a small
team of people who represented the interests of the Haitian government to the Bush administration and the Congress, and she had
arranged for Smiley to interview the president on Sunday, February
29, midday, at the National Palace. He was to be accompanied on his
turnaround charter by radio show host Tom Joyner, Princeton University religion professor Cornel West, and lawyer Raymond Brown, a
frequent guest host for Court TV. Hazel had exchanged e-mails and
spoken to Mildred Aristide by telephone earlier in the day. The
arrangements had been largely completed. The interview with Smiley

was to follow directly on the heels of a live ABC television interview conducted by George Stephanopoulous.

During the morning telephone call, Mrs. Aristide had said to Hazel that the president was looking forward to the Sunday interviews.

Hazel picked up the receiver.

"Hazel . . ." Tavis Smiley was a friend of ours. He hesitated before saying, "I have bad news."

"Oh no . . ."

"Tomorrow is off."

"Don't tell me. . . . Has something bad happened to them?"

"Well, Ron Dellums called me . . ." Former Democratic congressman Ron Dellums had been brought onto the Haiti team by Hazel two years before. ". . . and said that Colin Powell had just called to tell him that Guy Philippe and his men were coming tomorrow—Sunday—to kill President Aristide and that the United States will do nothing to help him."

"Oh my God! Randall has been trying all evening to reach the president and Mildred. He can't get through. . . . We have to get this out to the media right away. It's the only way to save them."

Hazel hung up the telephone and checked her voice mail for a message from Dellums. He had not called.

For days, Guy Philippe and his men had churned destructively through the open northern countryside where the government's lightly armed police had had little capacity to contain them. Philippe had boasted publicly that on Sunday, February 29, Philippe's birthday, he would come into Port-au-Prince and kill the president.

Although Mrs. Aristide had sent the children, Christine and Michaëlle, with a relative to Miami a few days before to stay with her parents for a school vacation visit, neither she nor the president, in the days before February 29, seemed unstrung by the building storm that appeared from the outside to be swirling around them. The foreign media, including the American media, had left the outside world with the unmistakable impression that by Saturday, February 28, the rebels were within easy striking distance of the capital, Port-au-Prince. Barbara Lee, the California Democrat who had taken Dellums's seat in Congress after his retirement, had even called Hazel to offer the assistance of the Congressional Black Caucus in finding a safe exit for the president and his wife.

Mrs. Aristide had been gracious as always when Hazel conveyed the congresswoman's offer.

"Please thank her for us, Hazel. But the president will not leave office until his term is completed. We will be fine." She then asked after the health and well-being of our family.

Mrs. Aristide's confidence seemed warranted by the public assurances Secretary of State Colin Powell had given that the United States would not allow a group of thugs to overthrow the democratically elected government of Haiti.

His statement followed assurances that he had given on February 13 to a meeting in Washington with representatives from CARICOM (Community of Caribbean States), France, Canada, and the Organization of American States that there would be no "regime change" in Port-au-Prince inasmuch as Aristide was the elected president of Haiti.

Five days later Agence Haitienne Press filed a story based on a statement released by James B. Foley, the U.S. ambassador to Haiti.

Port-au-Prince, February 18, 2004 -(AHP)- The U.S. Ambassador to Haiti, James B. Foley, warned Tuesday that the United States will not recognize any government that takes power through a coup d'état in Haïti.

James Foley asked the Haitian opposition to join in condemning the recent acts of violence experienced in the country.

Amb. Foley considers that one must move on from the logic of confrontation to that of dialogue under the auspices of the international community.

James B. Foley renewed the commitment of his government to work alongside CARICOM to find a peaceful solution to the crisis.

The American Ambassador invited the Haitian political actors to observe a truce in order to find the best formula for ending the crisis.

This call for a truce, said the U.S. diplomat, does not mean that the United States is seeking to maintain the status quo in Haiti. The idea is, he said, to have the necessary time to be able to make the changes the country needs.

Two days after Ambassador Foley's statement was released, Agence Haitienne Press reported that "a group of American military experts from the Southern Command" would soon arrive in Port-au-Prince.

Washington, February 19, 2004 -(AHP)- A group of American military experts from the Southern Command will arrive in Port-au-Prince within the next few day to evaluate the situation of American officials working in the country, a State Department leader declared.

The delegation will also work on a security plan in order to encourage Haitians to stay at home. Many citizens are facing serious security problems since the arrival of leaders of the terrorist group FRAPH, leading armed supporters of the opposition in Gonaïves.

According to the State Department official, the Pentagon is presently looking at the issue of security in Haiti in order to evacuate, if necessary, about 20,000 Americans living in Haiti.

The experts delegation will have work sessions with leaders of the United States Embassy in Port-au-Prince.

AHP February 19, 2004, 3:35 PM

Minutes after speaking with Tavis Smiley, Hazel called Ron Dellums. I was ten minutes before midnight on February 28.

"Ron, Tavis just called me. This is really awful."

"Yeah. The secretary [Powell] called me. He says that Guy Philippe is in Port-au-Prince. He's going to kill Aristide and the U.S. will do nothing to stop it."

"Ron, we have to call the media. We have to get this out! This is our only hope, or else they will kill them!"

Dellums neither supported nor opposed the suggested course of action. Silence ensued.

Hazel then called Ira Kurzban, who was general consul to the government of Haiti. For several years during the era of Haitian dictatorship preceding the election of Aristide, Kurzban, an American lawyer based in Miami, ably defended in American courts the immigration rights of Haitians seeking political refugee status in the United States.

"Ira, Tavis just called . . ." Hazel recounted to him what Secretary Powell had told Dellums. "We have to call the media. That's our only hope."

"Well . . . I don't know that we want to expose Ron. . . . "

"But they will kill them."

A scarcely audible reply betokened his ambivalence. It may have been understandable. None of us who were closely involved had more than minutes to think about what we were saying or deciding. In Hazel's case and mine, our decisions were likely driven more by desperation than anything else—as well as by a nearly paralyzing fear for the lives of two very decent human beings who had come to symbolize, for millions of Haitians, the right to rule themselves.

There was also the matter that Powell presumably had spoken to Dellums in confidence. There may have been a reluctance to compromise that confidence unnecessarily. Some of us, after all, may have been slow to believe that an black American secretary of state of Jamaican ancestry could stand by and allow (if not sanction) the murder of a black democratically elected head of state. But Powell had said the words directly to Dellums himself. Though naïveté does not die particularly hard, an entrenched infestation of it can certainly survive a shocking truth for more than minutes.

20

Basseterre, St. Kitts
Saturday, February 28, 2004, just before midnight

CALLED ABC WORLD NEWS TONIGHT AND ASKED for Peter Jennings. Someone at the news desk told me that he was away for the weekend. When I said I urgently needed to reach Jennings, I was assured that he would be located.

I then spoke with Randall Pinkston of *CBS News* and George Gedda of the Associated Press. After I described what Powell had said to Dellums, I was told they would have to speak with Dellums directly. I gave them a number where Dellums could be reached. Minutes later, Jennings called me from a social gathering he was attending. I went though the story again and gave him Dellums's number.

I placed my last call to Janice O'Connell in Washington, a senior foreign policy adviser to Senator Christopher Dodd (D-CT), a leading voice on Haiti. I gave O'Connell much the same information I had given to the journalists.

Within thirty minutes, Pinkston, Gedda, Jennings called to tell me that Dellums had declined to confirm his comments to Hazel and Smiley regarding what Powell had told him. No story would run. Hazel, the outside world, and I were now completely cut off from President and Mrs. Aristide. For the next thirty-six hours, all we could do was wait, worry, and pray.

●   ●   ●

For the uninitiated, Haiti must appear to be a bewildering stew of obscure and violent events, a homogeneously black place that is mired in arcane routines of chronic instability and engulfed in bloody internecine conflicts from which no one emerges unscathed. The good and the well-meaning are indistinguishable from the venal and self-seeking.

Grisly pictures spread across the Internet showing bodies in the streets. A New World African culture is parodied unsparingly. "Voodoo economics," says Ronald Reagan, having his turn. St. John Bosco, President Aristide's old parish church, is a burned-out hulk. An honorable and promising justice minister lies dead on a public street in a pool of thickening blood. Aristide, the brilliant humanitarian priest, twice overwhelmingly elected president by the poor, is described in an Internet tract as a vicious totalitarian dictator.

The distortions build into a fog continuously generated by faceless men in small meetings. On the ground beneath the fog, however, Haiti is quite comprehensible. In the main, it is the victim of severe class conflict, exacerbated by the kindred and derivative conflicts of color and culture.

To the ordinary news consumer, the relentless distortions justify just about anything, even the voiding of Haiti's democratic election, for instance. *Who gives a damn! They ain't our elections.*

Perhaps there is no campaign of cruelty more damnable than the sly sowing of a wasting untruth, American style. Master America—hugger-mugger propagator of the small vegetative cancerous lie that grows well in deep shade. The metronomic aspersions, however baseless, eventually have their effect. Even upon the Haitian New York taxi driver who had not too long ago said to me, "I'm beginning to wonder about Aristide . . ." tailing off dejectedly.

Think for a minute. Has there ever been a national leader anywhere in the world who tried to lift a people from poverty whom America did not oppose or even vilify? I cannot name even one.

The United States had begun the undoing of Aristide's reputation more than ten years before the event lying just ahead was triggered. In 1998, I wrote the following passage about Aristide in *Defending the Spirit*:

> How different he is from all that is said about him in American papers, where he has been variously described as a power-hungry lunatic and a communist. This public picture of him, which bears not the slightest resemblance to the man I know, is the inventive work of Brian Latelle, CIA Latin American station chief. Latelle claimed in a report circulated in Congress that Aristide had been treated for a mental illness (which he never suffered) at a Canadian hospital (to which he had never been) where he was treated by a certain doctor (who never existed). Of course the report was thoroughly disproved, but by then the thoroughly intended damage had been done.

Over the course of our lives, few of the people we hear about in the media, will we ever know, or for that matter, even meet. What we *hear*, that is, what little we get to read or learn from television or radio, will constitute the whole of what we get to know about the vast majority of those whose names we recognize.

We are all, to one degree or another, gullible. Generally, we believe what one person we do not know tells us about another person we do not know. We believe things that are told to us without knowing anything about the teller or the teller's motives for telling us things in the first place. We believe such unverified things, I think, because human beings somehow need to delude themselves in order to handle the stress brought on by daily assaults of unprocessable new information. We are usually prepared to trust as long as the betrayal of that trust comes at the expense of someone else and not ourselves.

I read several newspapers a day. Although I have every logical reason to question the correctness of some of what I read, I do not.* If I did, I would not continue reading newspapers. I know that what I am reading is, as often as not, wrong, particularly in regard to subjective characterizations of influential figures, but I persevere, reading newspapers, magazines, and books written by persons I have never heard of.

Some truths, however, remain self-evident. Vicious dictators and totalitarian autocrats, for instance, are *not* twice elected president by

---

* Despite strong advice from the U.S. State Department that Americans not attend Haiti's bicentennial celebrations on January 1, 2004, Hazel, Maxine Waters, Sidney Williams, scholar Molefi Kete Asante, actor Danny Glover, and others from the United States joined the hundreds of thousands at the National Palace for the bicentennial celebrations. Lydia Polgreen of the *New York Times* described the same crowd as "small but enthusiastic." Polgreen's crowd size estimate would later, following complaints, be excised from the same *New York Times* story that would run on the Internet.

overwhelming majorities in open, free, and fair elections. Nor do dictators and totalitarians disband their armies, which is what Aristide did in December 1994 scarcely two months after returning from the first of his two exiles. Dictators *expand* their armies. And for obvious reasons (to protect their own wretched necks), dictators never cashier the armed louts who shoot at their fellow citizens.

Of all the public *Christians* I have known personally, Aristide led a life that emulated the implacable *Christ* whose sympathies for the poor Aristide had since childhood taken deeply to heart.

Indeed, it was Aristide's very sincerity (an odd trait in politics, where pragmatism is coin of the realm) that led him afoul of those whose strategic, economic, and political interests he challenged.

I was invited recently to speak at a black alumni gathering of Harvard Law School graduates. A third of my remarks were about Haiti and the fateful events of February 29, 2004. Later, back at my hotel, I sat over drinks with several of the lawyers who were attending the three-day conference. One, a partner in a major Chicago law firm, had once served on the board of an organization I directed. He had made himself into a wealthy, politically well-connected man. He was, further, a good person.

After toying distractedly for thirty minutes with my cocktail napkin and contributing little to shop conversation among the lawyers, I rose to leave. My old friend, with something gnawing at him, raised his voice to be heard down the length of the table, "Randall, you got to let go of this Haiti thing. I mean you've just got to let go." He then said the same thing with escalating passion.

I was saddened by what he had said and by the edge in his tone. Though hardly a critical thinker, he was a smart and savvy fellow, who, in this instance, had no notion of what he was talking about. But he was rock certain of his ground and he had stood it.

The tellers had wormed their way into my friend's tidy cerebrum and left him inexplicably angry with *me* for raising a subject that white mainstream American tellers had packaged to him as little more than a *black mess*, or what American officials more clinically like to call a *failed state*.

Haiti, as a topic of concern, was a sore area for my friend, who simply believed, without reflection, everything he had been told. I don't think I ever could have shaken his conviction that Aristide and his government had destroyed themselves.

This is the shadowy way the Brian Latelles of the world poison public sentiment against democratic leaders and causes while they divert attention from the difficulties that face so many new and struggling democracies. The United States fomented malicious mischief against Haiti while we looked the other way, asked the wrong questions, and received the intentionally irrelevant answers.

21

CONVERGENCE HADN'T MUSTERED A COHERENT
point of view. Its members, brought together by the International Republican Institute, could not agree on anything save the president's ouster. New elections were the last thing that Convergence and Group 184 wanted. They knew that the Haitian people would reject them roundly. Although the president knew the Americans were telling everyone that the rebels were coming to Port-au-Prince on Sunday to kill him, he did not believe this. The Americans wanted to frighten him into leaving the country, thus causing him to lose face with the millions who had placed their trust in him. (Presumably American officials believed that a "voluntary" departure by the broadly supported president would demoralize the Haitian poor, thus making them more manageable and amenable to American direction.) In the hours before they

vanished, the president and his wife declared several times to several people that they would not leave Haiti. Moreover, they saw no reason to leave.

22

Airborne above Cap-Haïtien
Saturday, February 21, 2004, late afternoon

FRANTZ GABRIEL PILOTED THE ONLY AIRCRAFT that the Haitian government had use of—a leased forty-year-old Bell "Huey" helicopter that was used largely to fly medivac operations and to transport police and government ministers around the mountainous, often impassable countryside.

Gabriel was a sixty-year-old Haitian citizen who had served in Vietnam in 1967 as a sergeant in the U.S. Army's 11th Cavalry Black Horse Division.

Hearing rumors that the rebels had begun marching south toward Port-au-Prince to kill the president and seize control of the country, Gabriel flew the Huey north to Gonaïves and located the rebels on the ground moving slowly north toward Cap-Haïtien and *away* from the capital.

Days later, Secretary of State Colin Powell would give Ron Dellums, the former chairman of the House Armed Services Committee, bad information.

Still, the democratic government that had removed the makeshift barricades had nothing it could use to defend itself. A package of small arms, ammunition, and bulletproof vests en route from South Africa had arrived in Jamaica and was being processed for transshipment to Port-au-Prince. The president had declined to take the American bait. The arms would soon be leaving Jamaica for Haiti. American officials had to know its exact whereabouts. Events were not unfolding as they had hoped.

23

Renaissance Jaragua Hotel, Santo Domingo, Dominican Republic
Monday, March 29, 2004

HAVANA, March 29, 2004 (Xinhuuanet)

The United States armed and trained in the Dominican Republic the groups that rose against former Haitian President Jean-Bertrand Aristide, a preliminary report issued in the Dominican Republic indicated Monday.

This provisional conclusion was reached by the Investigation Commission on Haiti, formed by religious persons, lawyers of several nations and created in 1991 by the former U.S. attorney general Ramsey Clark.

"200 soldiers of the U.S. Special Forces arrived in the Dominican Republic with the authorization of Dominican Republic President Hipolito Mejia, as a part of the military operation to train Haitian rebels," declared the commission when unveiling the report in the Dominican capital, Santo Domingo. Priest Luis Barrios and lawyer Brian Concannon, both members of the "independent" Commission, presented the preliminary results of the investigation that contradicted the Dominican authorities which had previously considered "surrealistic and oneiric" the delivery of U.S. guns to Haitian rebels on their national soil, as some accusations stated.

A member of the Commission, Teresa Gutierrez, wondered "how the rebel leaders could train and arm in the Dominican Republic if the government of Mejia assured several times to his Haitian counterpart Aristide that he would tolerate no guerilla movement" in his territories.

Barrios said at a press conference that the commission had a "countless number of reports" proving that the Haitian rebels were armed and trained in Dominican military camps located in the eastern locality of San Isidro and the western regions of Haina and Neiba.

They also mentioned that rebel Guy Philippe was detained twice but "immediately released" in the Dominican Republic, in December 2001 and May 2003, while the insurgent leader Louis-Jodel Chamblain "was photographed" disguised as a Dominican police.

The most scandalous case was the release of the Haitian rebel Jean Robert after his followers kidnapped 16 Dominican soldiers in the northwestern province of Dajabon on February 14.

None of Aristide's foes, including the armed rebels, ever argued that he had committed an impeachable offense. No one could deny that he was the fairly elected head of a constitutional democratic government.

His enemies simply wanted him out, knowing that a new election (which Aristide welcomed) would only demonstrate their own lack of public support. Thus they were prepared to scuttle a democracy, a constitution, an elected parliament, a functioning national government, to drive one man—Jean-Bertrand Aristide—out of office, out of Haiti, indeed, out of the Western Hemisphere.

For all of them—the hegemonic Americans and the obedient Dominicans they directed; the brutish, semiliterate rebels who held the childlike belief that they, in the end, would be delivered of the small-place power they so glandularly craved; the French who'd managed throughout a checkered history to come to terms with every national humiliation, save the one handed to them two hundred years before by Toussaint L'Ouverture, a black former slave; the rich Francophile Haitian whites and the fractional blacks who took and took, oblivious to the suffering of those they exploited— Aristide brought to the responsibilities of his office a disturbing combination of traits and abilities.

He was sharp-witted and creative, authoring ten books and composing music for six instruments—guitar, saxophone, organ, drums, clarinet, and piano.

He was a priest who was uncommonly self-possessed and principled. He had been born black and poor, a *peyizan* who loved the peasantry as he had his mother, his father, and the millions like them.

"He was espousing change in Haiti, fundamental populist change," said Robert Maguire, a foreign policy scholar at Trinity University in Washington, D.C. "Right away, he was viewed as a threat by very powerful forces in Haiti."

He had begun to talk about and move publicly toward building a more equitable relationship between the haves who'd always had their way and the have-nots, who, in this slight figure of a man, had found a voice. He wanted to change Haiti and he set about doing just that. His enemies, however, would stop at nothing to rid the country of him and the aspirations of the millions he represented.

To this wholly illegal and antidemocratic purpose, several forces cleaved as one—the armed rebels, the United States of America, France, Canada, the Dominican Republic, and a new association of Haitian opposition splinter groups forged, funded, and counseled by the International Republican Institute, the Convergence Democratique, which would later morph into a subversive organ known as Group 184.

●　　●　　●

The Investigation Commission on Haiti presented its findings on Monday, March 29, 2004, one month after Aristide was deposed, to an audience of more than one hundred journalists who had crowded into a meeting room in the Renaissance Jaragua Hotel in Santo Domingo, Dominican Republic.

Dr. Luis Barrios, A New York–based Catholic priest speaking for the commission, read from a prepared statement:

> Our investigation so far has proven some facts beyond a doubt, and established others as likely. . . . First, there is no doubt that the territory of the Dominican Republic was used for training and arming the Haitian rebels, with the knowledge of the national authorities (government of the

Dominican Republic), and that their attack was launched from Dominican soil. This is proven by several facts: The rebel leader Guy Philippe operated out of the territory from late 2000 until last month, when he launched his violent attack. Other rebel leaders did as well, including: Joel Chamblain, the number two leader of Haiti's largest paramilitary organization, and a convicted murderer; former army captain Ernst Ravix; Paul Arcelin, reportedly responsible for raising money for the rebellion and for Haiti's political opposition [Convergence]. Mr. Philippe has been openly working to overthrow the Haitian government since 2000. . . .

President Mejia (Dominican Republic) told a journalist we spoke with that 'Guy Philippe is under my control', and that President Aristide's concern with Philippe was 'an obsession'. . . . Jodel Chamblain has been photographed wearing a Dominican army uniform with a *Policia National* insignia. . . . U.S. military officials have confirmed that 20,000 M16 rifles were given by the U.S. to the Dominican Republic after November 2002, and admitted that many of these rifles were now in the hands of the Haitian rebels. . . . Two hundred (American) Special Forces soldiers came to the Dominican Republic as part of "Operation Jaded Task", with special authorization from President Mejia. We have received many reports that this operation was used to train Haitian rebels. We have many consistent reports of Haitian rebel training centers at or near Dominican military facilities. These include San Ysidro, Haina, San Cristobal, Hatillo, Neiba. . . .

It is clear that the Dominican Republic was also used by the United States to support the political opposition in Haiti, which was linked to the violent opposition. Once a month, the U.S. government's International Republic [sic] Institute held meetings for the Haitian opposition leaders in Santo Domingo, usually at the Hotel Santo Domingo. One of those regularly attending meetings was Paul Arcelin, the spokesman for Haiti's opposition platform, the Convergence Democratique, in the Dominican Republic, the self-described head of the political arm of the rebels, and reportedly the rebel's principle fundraiser.

24

Los Angeles, California
Sunday February 29, 2004, 1:15 P.M. PST

"HELLO." HAZEL'S VOICE WAS FLAT WITH EX-haustion. We had lain awake for most of the night.

"Hazel? Max. Have you heard anything?" It was Maxine Waters calling from California.

"Nothing. Nothing at all," Hazel said.

"Have you been watching CNN? They're saying that the president and Mildred fled the country last night. I don't believe it. I talked to them yesterday about the Sunday interview with Tavis. They weren't going anywhere."

No one ever accused the Democratic representative from south-central Los Angeles of being mealy mouthed. Quite unlike a successful New York official who had once said famously to a friend in crisis, "I'll support you *as long as I can*," Waters fought indefatigably for the causes and people she believed in. Her fearless style evoked either favor or disfavor, but seldom indifference. Hazel and I liked her immensely.

"There was one thing. . . . We don't know yet that it means anything."

"What is it?"

"We got a phone call from an official in Antigua asking for our fax number. The official wanted to fax us the customs declaration for an American plane that arrived in Antigua in the middle of last night and sat, after refueling, for hours in a remote corner of the airport before taking off early this morning. The official sounded frustrated and said that the U.S. declaration form misrepresented what was on the plane. The Antiguan airport ground officials were prevented from boarding the aircraft by the Americans.

"The plane was large and white and had no tail number. An oversize American flag on the vertical section of the tail assembly was the only identification mark that the plane bore. He said that the windows didn't look like cargo plane windows, you know that blanked-out painted-over look. They looked like the windows in a passenger plane with the shades drawn.

"The customs declaration claimed that the plane was coming from Guantanamo, Cuba."

"Have they faxed it to you yet?"

"No, not yet."

They fell silent. Waters was the most ardent defender of Haiti's fragile young democracy in Congress. In the time between the bicentennial celebration of January 1, 2004, and the events of February 29, two months later, she turned up in Haiti with considerable frequency. She worried over the intrigues of Group 184, which supported any extrajudicial methods, including those employed by the treasonous rebels with whom they were in league, that would result in the president's summary ouster from the country. She was also troubled by the sharp discrepancy between the widespread popular support expressed for the president inside Haiti and the harshly disparaging picture given of him to the outside world by American news organizations. Indeed, Americans were being led to *disremember* that Aristide had been elected lawfully—twice. Further, there were no charges of malfeasance, either adjudicated or formally lodged against him. Where Haiti was concerned, Americans in general were demonstrating a growing taste for mob methods of political transition, methods that Americans would never knowingly countenance for themselves at home. It was as if the Haitian people, together with the 7,500 officials they had democratically elected, counted for nothing. It had become painfully clear that to Americans, Haitians were little more than valueless pieces on a game board. They could be scuttled at the pleasure of the State Department, which expected elected officials in poor black countries like Haiti to resign on Washington's command the offices to which their own people had elected them.

● ● ●

By February 2004, the rebels, this time three hundred strong and bearing American arms, again came marauding into Haiti, torching fire stations and jails, releasing criminals from their cells, and murdering rural police officers.

Days before the country reached bottom, with the north in flames, Waters learned that Roger Noriega, U.S. assistant secretary of state for Latin America and former senior adviser to Senator Jesse Helms, was traveling to Haiti to meet with President Aristide. The congresswoman guessed that Noriega, in the wake of the mushrooming rebel violence that the United States had indirectly instigated, was going to Port-au-Prince to tell President Aristide that it was time for him to leave, just as the French foreign minister's sister had done a short time before. Inoculating the scheme against charges of racism was the responsibility of Foreign Minister Fred Mitchell of the Bahamas, a Caricom member country that enjoyed a reputation of being something of a lickspittle for Noriega in the region.

When Representative Waters and Ambassador Williams walked into the boarding area of the Miami International Airport for the flight to Port-au-Prince, Mitchell became visibly distressed. His discomposure deepened when Waters told him that she was also going to Port-au-Prince and would be on the American Airlines flight with him and Noriega.

At the Toussaint L'Ouverture Airport in Haiti, Mitchell, the Bahamian foreign minister, was met by a driver from the U.S. embassy. Waters and Williams, in contrast, rode into the city in an overworked Nissan provided by the Haitian government. The two went directly to the president's office at the National Palace, where a meeting was about to begin between President Aristide and the Noriega–Mitchell team. Waters, who had long before earned the trust of President Aristide, entered the room with her husband, sat down, and introduced herself to Noriega and Mitchell (who already knew her all too well) as a member of the U.S. Congress with a "special interest in U.S.–Haiti relations."

Neither Noriega nor Mitchell wanted her in the room and attempted a number of maneuvers to get her out. None of them worked. The congresswoman had reason to believe that something untoward was planned for that weekend in Haiti and had she not been there, it would have been carried out. She was all but certain that Noriega, on instruction from Secretary of State Colin Powell, and with the tacit approval of the obsequious Mitchell, had come from Washington to order President Aristide to exit his office and leave his country.

In a matter of days, her intuition, at least about Washington's overall objective, would prove close to the mark.

● ● ●

"Have you and Randall heard anything about the whereabouts of the package?" the congresswoman asked Hazel over the telephone.

The *package* was how we, for weeks, had referred cryptically on the phone to a shipment of police supplies from South Africa that, as events developed, did not arrive in time to help the overmatched Haitian police force defend the country and its democracy. The package was to have included an undisclosed amount of small arms, ammunition, and protective gear for the police.

In the months before, the Haitian government had next to nothing it could use to repulse the rebels bearing American M16s, M50s, and grenade launchers.* The people, however, rallied in defense of their government, mounting an elaborate system of tire barricades,

---

* During the most recent period of military dictatorship (1991–1994), the Clinton administration imposed an embargo on the sale of weapons and ammunition to the military rulers who had overthrown President Aristide in 1991. The embargo was not lifted by the United States when Aristide and democracy was restored in October 1994. The Bush administration refused to lift the embargo when the government of Haiti was being threatened by armed rebels in early 2004. Immediately following the ouster of President Aristide and 7,500 elected officials in late February and early March of 2004, the Bush administration lifted the embargo to permit the provision of weapons to an unelected foreign-installed "government."

trucks, and boulders across roads leading to the palace. Hundreds of thousands stood at the ready to jam the streets of Port-au-Prince.

While this may have been a practicable plan to defend Port-au-Prince, which the rebels could not have taken and held anyway, the lightly policed countryside remained nakedly vulnerable.

"Randall spoke to Zuma in Mumbai. She said the package will be reaching Jamaica any minute now."

Dr. Zuma was South Africa's foreign minister. In an effort to reach her, I had called London to speak with Lindiwe Mabuza, an old friend from the antiapartheid campaign years, who was South Africa's ambassador to Great Britain. Ambassador Mabuza located foreign minister Zuma in India attending a ministerial conference.

Although I had never met the foreign minister, I had reason to believe that she would also be worried about what was happening to Haiti's democracy. After all, she had likened Haiti's dilemma to that faced by black South Africans during apartheid. But her vision of the significance of Haiti for blacks globally was larger than any perceived similarities between Haiti's anguish and South Africa's under apartheid.

25

Black Haitians are singled out by America from their black Caribbean neighbors for special animus, at least in part because Haitians are not only black, but, to American eyes, culturally distinguishable (indeed stubbornly so), unaccountably proud of themselves, and, it would seem, unmanipulable as well. For American and European policymakers, Aristide symbolized all of this. This was likely what President Chirac really meant when he said that he didn't like Aristide, a convivial, smart, self-possessed man with his own ideas for his own people.

This alone was cause enough for American and French officials to act against him. Goethe's old warning seemed as fresh as yesterday: "Beware of those in whom the urge to punish is powerful."

For the record, whether an elected official, in America or anywhere else, is *liked* or *disliked* carries no constitutional weight whatsoever, except on the occasion of an election. No working democracy exists on earth in which there are not, in absolute terms, large numbers of people who dislike those whom clear majorities lawfully and democratically elect. This does not mean that, *in a democracy*, disgruntled minorities are entitled to tear up a society, constitution, and country in order to produce a change of government that the constitution provides ample democratic opportunity for.

In the case of Haiti, the United States and the powerful Haitian insurrectionists it supported cared little or nothing about the requirements of Haiti's democratic constitution. They wished only to crush the reform-minded government of a democratically elected president, and, with him, all hope in the years ahead for constitutional democracy in Haiti. To America, the ensuing hellish, bloody turmoil associated with its lawless interposition seemed less a collateral consequence of Washington's support for the coup d'état than a fully intended outcome of the overall American strategy.

Harold Pinter, the English writer and 2005 Nobel Prize winner for literature, might well have had America's role in the destabilization of Haiti's democracy in mind when he prepared the Nobel lecture he delivered in December 2005:

> Direct invasion of a sovereign state has never in fact been America's favored method. In the main, it has preferred what it has described as "low intensity conflict". Low intensity conflict means that thousands of people die but slower than if you drop a bomb on them in one full swoop. It means that you can infect the heart of the country, that you establish a malignant growth and watch the gangrene bloom. When the populace has been subdued—or beaten

to death—the same thing—and your own friends, the military and the great corporations, sit comfortably in power, you go before the camera and say democracy has prevailed.

26

Los Angeles, California
Sunday, February 29, 2004, 1:20 P.M. PST

OUR TELEPHONE CONVERSATION WITH MAXINE Waters on the afternoon of February 29, 2004, twelve hours after Aristide disappeared, slowed to silence. After a point, none of us knew what more to say. The president of Haiti and his wife had vanished. All we knew with certainty was that they had not "fled," as official American sources were claiming and world news organizations were regurgitating as an incontrovertible fact. Though no one on us said as much, we feared that they had been killed.

Sick with worry, we worked to stay our sinking spirits by finding matters, by then well moot, to talk about.

"What happened with the Regional Security Service?" asked Waters. "Would P.J. know what happened?"

"Maybe Ira has heard something."

On Thursday, February 26, two days before Haiti's government fell, Denzil Douglas, prime minister of St. Kitts and Nevis, had come out of a cabinet meeting to take Hazel's emergency call. She asked him about mobilizing the forces of the Caribbean Regional Security Service in Haiti's defense. The prime minister was empathetic and referred Hazel to Ralph Gonsalves, prime minister of St. Vincent and the Grenadines. Within the Caribbean community, Gonsalves had been, perhaps, the most outspoken defender of Haiti's democracy. Concerned, but lacking authorization to mobilize the force, Gonsalves gave Hazel the telephone number of the military official who commanded the force. When she spoke to the official, he listened politely. As we were shortly to learn, however, the Regional Security Service was in no position to move.

The service, comprised of the armed forces of Caribbean Community (Caricom) countries, was trained by the U.S. military and undertook joint Tradewinds military exercises. In addition, Caribbean soldiers were trained by the United States to perform natural disaster rapid response procedures, political crisis and social upheaval management, drug eradication and interdiction maneuvers.

27

Tabarre, Haiti
Friday, February 27, 6:00 P.M.

ON THE EVENING OF FRIDAY, FEBRUARY 27, as the president arrived by car at his home at Tabarre, the first of two gates giving onto Boulevard 15 Octobre was opened, as usual, by a familiar Haitian officer of the USGPN (Unité Specialisée de la Garde du Palais National). Accompanying the president in separate cars was a detail of security guards from the Steele Foundation, a private security firm based in San Francisco, California. The president appeared tired but smiled and exchanged salutations with a uniformed young Haitian man who stood erect in the small masonry-wall gatehouse. The Steele guards, resembling members of the American secret service, wore dark suits and somber ties. Their jackets concealed shoulder holsters and light pistols. En route, they had protected the president's three-car motorcade with a heavier short-barreled weapon that looked like a modified M16.

On the streets of the capital, the Steele Foundation men were conspicuous less for their conservative dress than for their white skin. While several of the agents had been black shortly after the president's predecessor, Rene Preval, contracted for their services in 1998, by the time of the coup d'état, they were an all-white force of former U.S. Special Forces soldiers, intelligence officers, and security experts.

The company's contract with the Haitian government had been approved by the U.S. Department of State before the beginning of the second of Aristide's two abbreviated presidencies.

After removing the barricades in Port-au-Prince and then learning of the rebels' continued unwillingness to talk, the president, seeing little choice, sought to increase the number of Steele Foundation guards beyond their usual few dozen. Shortly after that, the *Miami Herald* reported that U.S. officials had blocked Steele Foundation reinforcements from traveling to Haiti in the days before the president's disappearance.

According to Democracy Now, the Steele Foundation then "asked the U.S. embassy in Port-au-Prince on Saturday February 28 whether the company could count on American protection in the event of rebel hostilities at the Presidential Palace (sic). They were reportedly told that no such protection would be provided."*

With offices on five continents and representing itself as "the first organization in history to be hired directly by a sovereign nation to provide full time protection for its Heads of State," the Steele Foundation

---

* Given what happened in the hours ahead, it seems unlikely that such an exchange ever occurred between the Steele Foundation and the U.S. embassy. Nothing in the understanding that the discussants likely shared would have necessitated it. Or at least this was the view of many close to the government who, after the disappearance of the president and his wife, came to believe that Steele had been given an early heads-up by American officials about what was to happen in the early hours of February 29.

had a prominent presence wherever American interests lay. In Iraq, by the spring of 2004, the company had five hundred people on the ground providing security for American wartime reconstruction projects.

The president's car passed through the second gate and drew into a large, landscaped yard. Folding chairs and round lunch tables were being stacked and carried from the lawn. The car moved around a horseshoe driveway and stopped before a walkway that led into an attractive masonry-clad house. The Steele Foundation vehicles turned right off the driveway and into a parking lot on the property reserved for Haitian government and Steele Foundation personnel.

On Friday afternoons, fifty or more poor children from hardscrabble neighborhood streets and from Lafanmi Selavi (the Family Is Life school for disadvantaged children that the president founded in 1986 while still a priest) came to the home for lunch and discussion and splash-play in the swimming pool. Madame Lucien, a superb cook, would have a hot meal ready before the children arrived with their favorite counselor, Mèt Dorcé, on two aging buses.*

On weekends it is the kids from *Lafanmi Selavi* who came to our house to spend time, to share food, talk, play and swim in the swimming pool. It is a small pool, too small for four hundred kids, but for them it is a place of paradise. Sometimes we invite other children; restavèk,† children from parishes in *Port-au-Prince*; sometimes a *Lafanmi Selavi* bus goes to *Cité Soleil*, to *La Saline*, to *Carrefour* to pick up children

---

* *Mèt* is the Kreyol word which describes the formal title of *teacher*. Mèt Dorcé was not a teacher but the title was used with his name as a demonstration of respect.

† *Restavèk* in a Kreyol word meaning "stay with," which describes the plight of children who live in virtual bondage with wealthy families.

who want to swim. This experience, which may appear at first as merely symbolic, has tremendous ramifications. In a country where only twenty per cent of the population have access to clean drinking water, swimming pools are exclusively for the rich. There is not a single public swimming pool in Haiti. The pool itself is a symbol of the elite.

We know the kids need food, we know they need school, but we cannot give all of them these things in a day. So while we are working to change the society, we can give them a day in a swimming pool. We say no child is so poor she does not deserve to swim in a pool. And if you imagine this has no impact on the society, think again.

The kids swim with us, with their teachers, with a group of agronomists who work with them on Saturdays, and with American friends and volunteers working at *Lafanmi Selavi*. A mix of races and social classes in the same water. Sometimes images have appeared on television. Shortly after we began this experience we started hearing reports from friends among the upper classes of rumors that I was preparing these "vagabon", these street children, to invade their swimming pools. Were it not tragic it would be comic. Perhaps the real root of the fear is this; if a maid in a wealthy home sees children from *Cité Soleil* swimming in a swimming pool on television, she may begin to ask why her child cannot swim in the pool of her boss.

So it is a system of social apartheid that we are questioning. We saw the same phenomena during the civil rights movement in the United States where attempts to integrate beaches and swimming pools met with some of the worst violence of the period. The same was true in

South Africa. What we are facing in Haiti is a form of apartheid. . . . The polarizations are many: literate/illiterate; rich/poor; black/white; male/female; those who have clean water to drink/those who don't. In Haiti, where these polarities remain so strong, swimming in the same water has both psychological and social repercussions. You swim with people you are close to. If you are a family, if you are a community, swimming together may improve the quality of the relationship. Our experience has shown that the water can help to melt the barriers between us, and wash away the dirt of prejudice.

JEAN-BERTRAND ARISTIDE
Eyes of the Heart

The weekly Friday event was overseen by Mildred Aristide, who, in the early afternoon, would start for home from her office in the National Palace from which she chaired Haiti's National HIV/AIDS Commission. Before chairing the commission, she had worked with human rights lawyers from an office at 168 John Brown Avenue.*

---

* John Brown Avenue is one of the most important and heavily traveled streets in Port-au-Prince. The street was named in honor of American abolitionist John Brown after he was hanged on December 2, 1859, with four co-conspirators (two of whom were black, Shields Green and John Copeland) after attempting to end American slavery by undertaking an armed raid on the federal armory at Harpers Ferry, West Virginia. After the execution, flags in Haiti were flown at half-mast and a special mass was held at the cathedral in Port-au-Prince where Haitian President Fabre Nicholas Geffard spoke of Brown's efforts against slavery in laudatory terms. The Haitian newspapers *Le Progrès* and *Feuille de Commerce* gave large coverage to Brown's trial and execution. The great black abolitionist Frederick Douglass, who knew and respected Brown, was to say of him, "If John Brown did not end the war that ended slavery, he did at least, begin the war that ended slavery." In no country in the world has the memory of John Brown been more revered than in Haiti.

28

MILDRED ARISTIDE WAS BORN MILDRED Trouillot in New York City to Haitian-born parents in 1962. Attractive and brilliant, she graduated in 1984 summa cum laude in urban legal studies from City College of New York and earned a law degree from the University of Pennsylvania Law School.

She met Jean-Bertrand Aristide while serving as legal adviser to the constitutional government of Haiti during the president's exile in the United States following the first coup d'état, which drove him and his democratic government from office on September 30, 1991. After democracy was restored on October 15, 1994, she moved to Haiti where she and the president were married on Saturday, January 20, 1996, in a ceremony at Tabarre attended by a gathering that included several Catholic priests from Haiti's human rights community.

Monsignor Wily Romélus, the Catholic bishop from Jérémie, presided at the wedding. The elderly prelate had been soft-spoken but fearless in his opposition to the dictator Jean-Claude Duvalier.

During the 1991–1994 coup, Monsignor Romélus had been beaten severely on the steps of the Port-au-Prince Cathedral. He later became godfather to the Aristides' first daughter, Christine. Also present was respected priest Father Adrien, as well as a much younger cleric named Gerard Jean-Juste, a founding member of the Haitian Refugee Center in Miami. Anthony Lake, the national security adviser to President Clinton was there, as well as William Swing, the U.S. ambassador to Haiti. Interspersed with the luminaries were children from Lafanmi Selavi, the school for street children founded by Aristide.

29

Port-au-Prince, Haiti
Mid-February 2004

WITH COUP RUMORS FLYING EVERYWHERE, THE capital city ground to a standstill. There remained, however, work to be done.

Three hundred thousand Haitians were sick with AIDS. The National Commission, chaired by Mildred Aristide, had done a remarkable job, particularly considering that the United States had blocked the health loans that the Inter-American Development Bank had long since approved for its work. This was doubly heartless, given that American men were overrepresented among the sex tourists walking the Champs de Mars soliciting Haitian men and boys. The thirty-member commission met monthly at the National Palace. The business members, in the climate of coup rumors, had boycotted the January meeting because of their "opposition" to government policies, a catchall pretext for fighting anything the government was trying to accomplish.*

Ten months after the president's disappearance, the director of United Nations AIDS acknowledged in his World AIDS Day Message that AIDS infections in Haiti had dropped between 1995 and 2004, a period that was almost exactly coterminous with the duration of democracy in Haiti.

In 2001, Mildred Aristide led a Haitian delegation of public and private sector representatives to the United Nations Special General Assembly on AIDS. It was during that meeting that the Global Fund for AIDS, Tuberculosis, and Malaria was instituted. Following on the U.N. meeting, the government of Haiti, in early 2002, submitted a proposal for funding to the newly established Global Fund. The proposal was developed by the Haitian government's Ministry of Health and a number of nongovernmental organizations, including Partners in Health, a group headed by Dr. Paul Farmer, the Harvard Medical School professor associated with Université Populaire.

In compliance with Global Fund requirements, Haiti's National AIDS Commission made itself over into a Country Coordinating

---

* The government was democratic, which meant that it was overwhelmingly black and formed from the poorer classes. The idea of democracy in Haiti was new. The exactingly inelastic bond of class allegiance, however, was not. In fact, the impediments to compromise and reconciliation between the opposing classes and colors of Haitian society were virtually as robust in early 2004 as they had been during the age of slavery. The allegiances were so strong that they even appeared to govern the views of Haitians who had been living outside the country for years and, in some cases, even decades.

Carl Fombrun, 74, was a fair-skinned society columnist, socialite, and longtime prominent member of South Florida's community of upwardly mobile Haitian professionals. When his well-to-do peers demanded that Aristide resign his presidency, Fombrun would not go along with them: "I was called a traitor to my class."

Mechanism (CCM), and by late 2002 it won approval from the fund for its proposal, as well as high marks for its work.

Besides the direct funding obstructions mounted by the Bush administration, there were other impediments to the CCM's work that had to be overcome or outmaneuvered.

When former U.S. President Bill Clinton laid on plans in 2003 to travel to Haiti for the signing of a protocol of agreement with the government to help raise money to combat AIDS in Haiti, the Bush administration fought tooth and nail to stop his visit. After it lost that battle, it then fought against holding the signing ceremony in a Haitian government building. (The event eventually went forward at the State University Hospital.)

In the summer of 2003, the Global Fund invited Mrs. Aristide to address a major conference on AIDS it was holding in France, but was forced to disinvite her after the French government blocked her participation in the conference.

On still another occasion, when preparing to speak about AIDS at one of the many public high schools to which the CCM had carried its AIDS campaign, she asked the UNICEF representative in Haiti for Kreyol-language pamphlets on AIDS to hand out to the students. She was told that UNICEF had no AIDS literature in Kreyol, causing her to question what UNICEF could have been doing about AIDS in Haiti (which was not a French-speaking country, but a Kreyol-speaking country) without so much as a page of AIDS prevention information in Kreyol.

No step taken to reduce the country's AIDS infection rate was easily accomplished under such politically rancorous circumstances. Virtually every measure the CCM took was contested by the United States. But Haitian officials persevered productively by applying the

Global Fund's assistance prudently, and by maximizing the use of meager local resources that, despite the painful financial embargo, remained under the government's control. No action or strategy was too small to consider. The CCM painstakingly evaluated them all and tried its best to implement the most promising ones.

Frantz Gabriel was placed at the disposal of Partners in Health to transport in the noisy Huey to Cange in the Central Plateau, Haiti's first CD4 cell counter. (The machine's sensitive setting would never have withstood the difficult overland passage.)

The machine had been shipped to Haiti from Boston. Dr. Farmer describes the machine's use:

> In order to "stage" people with HIV disease—in order to determine who most needs antiretroviral treatment—it is necessary to have a complex and fragile laboratory instrument called a CD4 cell counter. There were, at the time, none in rural Haiti. Doctors from Harvard met in Cange, in the middle of Haiti's Central Plateau, and shook hands with First Lady Mildred Aristide on a deal that would make AIDS care as good there as anywhere else in the world:
>
> They would procure a CD4 counter and she would have it transported by helicopter to the football pitch in front of the hospital. This was the beginning of the poor world's largest rural scale-up program.

After the fall of the government, Laurie Garrett wrote in a *New York Times* op-ed piece that "as chaotic as it is, Haiti surpassed its 2006 targets after only a year of Global Fund support."

Information about AIDS prevention was integrated into classroom materials in the country's public high schools. A system was set up to expedite the movement of AIDS medicines through Haitian customs for swift delivery to the ill. The School for Midwives was reopened. A school lunch program was instituted, as well as a school bus program with buses bearing on their side panels the word *Dignity*. Hôpital de la Paix, a state-of-the-art teaching hospital, was inaugurated on February 6, 2004, just three weeks before the government was brought down.

The normalization of diplomatic relations with Cuba on February 6, 1996 (the last day of President Aristide's first presidential mandate) facilitated the later deployment across Haiti of five hundred Cuban health care workers—doctors, nurses, and lab technicians. Haitian doctors went to Cuba to be trained and Cuban doctors came to Haiti to teach at the Université Populaire.

Existing clinics and hospitals were upgraded. Literacy programs were initiated in some places and expanded in others. For the first time in memory, the common people of Haiti were experiencing, albeit modestly, what it felt like to be *served* by a government. Yet there remained major inadequacies in the health care delivery system, most of which the government had little material wherewithal to address. Where it could make a difference, however, it appeared to be trying industriously to do so.

The country's insufficient blood supply, for example, had long been a major problem. Surgical candidates in Haiti traditionally had to secure their own blood supply before undergoing surgery. In 2003, Mildred Aristide started a campaign to promote an awareness among Haitians of the need to donate blood. Surgical candidates who were poor and without means to secure their own supply of blood were dying for lack of as little as a liter of blood. There had existed in Haiti no tradition of blood gifting. Mildred Aristide began to emphasize publicly that blood giving in a poor country like Haiti had to be viewed as a community obligation. The president's wife reguarly went to Red Cross offices in Port-au-Prince to donate blood.

> Haiti faces the worst HIV/AIDS epidemic in the Western Hemisphere. Across this small island nation an estimated three hundred thousand people—six percent of the adult population—live with HIV/AIDS. Last year, approximately thirty thousand Haitians died of the disease, the leading cause of death among sexually active adults and young people. Although Haiti is one of the poorest countries in the hemisphere the comprehensive rural health services it offers in its Central Plateau stand as exemplary models of HIV/AIDS care and treatment for other low- to middle-income countries around the world.
>
> *Global Fund website*

The Haitians who conceived and implemented the country's exemplary program for AIDS care and treatment—the president, officials of his democratic government, the members of Haiti's National AIDS Commission, the commission's chairperson, First Lady Mildred Aristide—are the same people whose reputations American officials traduced and sullied unmercifully before the world. This, after all, was the American way, its modus operandi, its customary bloodless opening salvo in the staging of the small elective conquest—the one-sided scuffle that netted little more for America than the short-lived rush relished by powerful but incomplete men.

Lies layered upon lies. All cleanly crafted. All impassively delivered. Shorn entirely of empathy. For empathy cannot exist without a preexisting recognition of the innately equal worth of people who are *different* from ourselves—different in the way they look, the way they worship, the way they negotiate life.

From birth, Americans are taught to believe that their nationality is superior to all other nationalities. White Americans are socialized subliminally to believe that they are superior en masse to the members of other races. Of course, generalizations are always dangerous and virtually impossible to sustain. Indeed, there are, likely, millions of reflective white Americans for whom such generalizations do not obtain. Most people, however, irrespective of race, are *not* reflective and do not think critically. They are lemmings obedient largely to the tide and social fashion of the particular moment.

In any case, Americans, for whatever reasons, had fenced themselves socially and culturally off from a respectful engagement with the better part of humanity—the brown, the black, the otherwise exotic—including the masses of Kreyol-speaking Haitians for whom Americans generally felt nothing or, worse, small contempt. Little wonder that they did, given all they had and had not been allowed to know about an artistic and gifted people whose history was as storied as any people's on earth.

30

Tabarre
Friday, February 27, 2004, 6:00 P.M.

THE PRESIDENT OPENED THE BACK DOOR OF the small sedan and stepped out onto the walkway. He wore eyeglasses and a conservative suit. He moved his gaze to the right toward the parking lot and found an unfamiliar Steele Foundation guard watching him somewhat less neutrally than one would expect from security personnel. The guard looked away as the president turned to walk toward the front door of the house where Mildred Aristide waited for him on the top step. They missed the sight and sounds of their daughters, Christine, seven, and, Michaëlle, five. The girls had gone to Miami, days before, to vacation with their grandparents, Carmelle and Emile Trouillot, Mildred's mother and father, who were now naturalized American citizens.

Like their father who composed and played music in a variety of idioms, Christine and Michaëlle demonstrated their father's gift for musicianship. He had become accustomed to hearing, when he came through the gates, one or the other of them practicing on the piano in the living room. The silence drew him back to the crisis that was closing in on the country.

"How did lunch go?" he asked distractedly as they turned into the house.

"I think they had a great time. Even Maryse is beginning to come out of her shell." Maryse was twelve and lived on the street. Today was the second time she'd come to the house.

"Have we found a place for her yet?" Sometime before, the president had turned over to others the management of Lafanmi Selavi.

"No, but soon I think. She put on a swimsuit today and played in the water with the others."

"Good." His spirits seemed to rise a bit.

She reached out and took his hand. They understood each other intuitively. It was if their souls were, if not indistinguishable, seamlessly compatible. Theirs had been more than a storybook romance. It was obvious to those who knew them well that they were indispensable friends. There were differences between them, of course, but nothing that mattered. In small social gatherings of friends, she may have talked about ideas that interested them most, such as social justice, with an infectious passion that gathered pace as she spoke. He, on the other hand, would always allow others to speak before he spoke, and then spoke quietly and evenly.

Until I saw a film of his sermons given in Kreyol, his first language, I'd even wondered how such a soft-spoken, self-effacing man could electrify the so-called dispossessed masses. Even without understanding a word of Kreyol, on hearing and seeing the sermon, I understood the power of his public personality. This side of him, however, never seemed to show itself in the day-to-day small-place conduct of the ordinary affairs of his life. This quiet quality of social unobtrusiveness was unusual in a figure so public as a head of state.

I have known many leaders over the years, and everyone of them seemed to suck the air out of a room as they entered. In this regard, in my experience, Aristide was almost unique. This would explain, why, with the exception of one or two others, Aristide was the only public person I wished to know as a friend. The fame that he came by was incidental to the social mission he had made of his life. His fame seemed not an end in itself.

I learned from something Mildred Aristide said to me just how strong their partnership was. She said that another belief that she and "Titide" shared was the sense that their meeting, marriage, and work together had been fated.*

Having grown up in the Bronx, Mildred Aristide, whose Kreyol needed practice when she arrived in Haiti to live, spoke English with an American accent: "I chose law school almost unthinkingly. I realized once I had met Titide that I had become a lawyer to work with the government of Haiti and to move on to my mission. I never wanted to practice law. I wanted to apply those skills to Haiti. The law experience helped me to write speeches, prepare reports, and present our position in meetings. In meetings with Americans

---

* Titide is the hypocorism by which the president has been known since childhood. The word *Titide* is a diminutive of Aristide, reflecting the president's small stature. In Kreyol it is spelled *Titid*.

and other officials abroad, I always wore my Haiti flag pin to avoid being mistaken."

•   •   •

The president sat down on the sofa, removed his glasses, and rubbed his eyes. "How is Soeur Anne coming along?" he asked.

Soeur Anne, sixtyish, dark-skinned, and hugely popular, was Haiti's most famous singer and a *mambo*, or priestess. She had recently undergone surgery at Canape Verte Hospital in Bois Vernas, where the president and his wife had visited her on a rainy January Friday following the procedure. Soeur Anne had returned to Haiti in 1994 with the restoration of democracy after living for many years in the United States. A strong Haitian nationalist, she brought audiences to tears with her a capella renditions of "Hallelujah pour Ayiti" (Thank God for Haiti).* She was seen broadly as a Lavalas *rouge* ("red") because of her strong support for the antipoverty efforts of the president's party. The elites detested her.

"She's up and around in her kaftans. She's probably doing more than she should be doing."

Soeur Anne's doctor had ordered six weeks of bed rest when she left the hospital. For more than a month, she had been at home in lower Delmas. Her house fell within the boundaries of the police precinct that Guy Philippe had commanded before he began his efforts to overthrow the government.

---

* *Ayiti* is the original name of the island that Christopher Columbus renamed Hispaniola after he established there in 1492 his first settlement in the Americas. *Ayiti* is an Arawak word meaning *land of many mountains*. The name evolved into the modern spelling of the word *Haiti*.

On the coffee table rested a copy of *Investir dans l'humain* (Investing in human beings). The book laid out the government's plan for ameliorating the country's gripping poverty. It would be the first time in Haiti's two-hundred-year history that an effort of this kind would be seriously attempted. The plan envisioned developing the country from the ground up. "We started at the base with the people," the president had said. The country had been divided into 365 rural sections, each to have, minimally, a primary school, a health clinic, and a business component, usually a cooperative of one sort or another, made workable by small loans and microcredits. The three components were to be mutually reinforcing. The black poor for the first time were to be given hope and a well-described role in the economic rescue of their country. Haiti had suffered from intractable illiteracy. Under the plan, raising the national literacy rate was to be an objective of primary importance.

Happy with things as they were (particularly the nearly limitless availability of cheap, unlettered black labor), the powerful white and mixed-race business community opposed the plan on principle, as well as virtually all other programs that the government undertook. Elites were discouraged by the invidious social prohibitions of their class from judging any government program on its merits alone. Race and class were the warped lenses through which they myopically measured every policy, every attitude, every living, laboring soul in Haiti. They were invariably heard to say with bigoted consistency: *You can't go there. You can't meet them. You can't support that. You'd be helping the government.* For the government was not to be helped under any circumstance, *ever*. This was the law of the landed, the moneyed, the white, the light, the destructively privileged, the Pétion-Ville socialite heard berating her black tile setter who, heaven forbid, had placed the pretty ceramic square slightly awry: "You're stupid! You smell! *Kongo!*"

Though Aristide represented the overwhelming majority of the Haitian people, for the high-born he was little more than a *peyizan*, a peasant from the outside.

For this small minority of privileged Haitians, American support never faltered. Washington had done everything in its power to guarantee the government's failure.

●　　●　　●

The president looked at the book on the coffee table. Everything had become terribly difficult. It was all slipping away. Though the vast majority of Haitians supported him and his government, he realized that for all strategic intents and purposes he was alone.

31

I N NOVEMBER 1984, I ASKED MARY FRANCES
Berry and Representative Walter Fauntroy to go with me to be
arrested at the South African embassy in a protest against apartheid.
They agreed immediately. Years later, I would ask a number of
prominent black Americans to join me in a hunger strike to protest
President Clinton's cruel and illegal repatriation of Haitian refugees
fleeing for their lives from the American-armed Haitian military dictatorship that had overthrown Haiti's first democratically elected
government. This time around, no one joined me and I had to under-
take a twenty-eight-day hunger strike alone.

News of the arrest at the South African embassy of three well-
known African Americans on November 21, 1984, went around the
world and was met with an explosion of spontaneous support from
thousands of African Americans. They came from every corner of
America to volunteer for arrest in the days, weeks, and months
following the jailing of Fauntroy, Berry, and me. Virtually the entire

Congressional Black Caucus went to jail. Maxine Waters, then a member of the California state legislature, led the campaign in California. The San Francisco Bay area's Ron Dellums, by then a veteran member of Congress, was one of the first to step forward in Washington. He joined me in jail the second time I spent a night there.

Despite the efforts of congressional representatives like John Conyers, Charles Rangel, and Barbara Lee, all of whom were arrested during the antiapartheid campaign, nothing that they or any of the rest of us tried in our effort to rally support for Haiti's democracy elicited from black Americans anything near the interest that black Americans had demonstrated during the long and successful antiapartheid movement. Democracy for black South Africans had been somehow more important, more compelling as an idea. African Americans had understood intuitively the first of the two calls to action. But they appeared, as a broadly inclusive community, not to have understood the second call at all.

Why?

African Americans, by and large, never saw what was happening in Haiti as a racial issue. Indeed, everything about the way that Haitian society had been described to Americans in general made it difficult to view Haiti's crisis in racial terms. Americans were given to believe that Haiti was an *all-black* society and that its wounds had been self-inflicted. What blacks do to one another has never galvanized black Americans into broad public action. Owing to blacks' long and lethal experience with slavery and its continuing aftermath, what *whites* do to blacks, quite understandably, preoccupies black Americans as an entire community.

White South Africans made a vociferous global boast of their claim to racial supremacy, and then, all in one very tribal white breath, enshrined the noxious idea in public law, while giving the corpus of their newly promulgated race-based restrictions a formal name: *apartheid.*

Rich whites and mulattoes in Haiti did not make a public political religion of their treatment of black Haitians in the way that white South Africans had in invoking the name of God to justify their treatment of South African blacks.

Both ruling minorities, however, used a comparatively small number of malleable blacks against their own black communities. In South Africa's case, blacks were used to help the white minority to forcibly relocate the country's black majority into worthless resource-poor homelands that blacks were to "lead," live in, and accept as their own "independent countries." More cleverly, the white and mixed-race ruling class in Haiti hid behind its black puppet dictators, so successfully that few in the outside world knew that Haiti had countless powerful families and interests that were *not* black.

Powerful American institutions, both public and private, either wittingly or unwittingly, assisted wealthy whites in Haiti in propagating this deception.

In a January 24, 2006, *New York Times* article about the descent and disarray of Haiti after the February 29 coup d'état, Ginger Thompson described Group 184 leader Andy Apaid as a "wealthy Haitian businessman who runs textiles factories. . . . The Aristide government was undone by a protest movement, led by people like the businessman, Mr. Apaid, a revolt by former soldiers and police officers and American pressure.

"They thought they could get rid of one government and have the country to themselves and their friends," a United Nations official said, asking not to be identified out of fear that his comments could hurt his position in Haiti."

Thompson's misleading description of what happened to Haiti leaves the reader with the impression of a society locked in the throes of a crippling internecine black-on-black Haitian-against-Haitian power struggle. As attested by seminal figures like Frederick Douglass and C. L. R. James, unabating racial discrimination, both foreign and domestic, is the very gravamen of the unredressed hurts that have torn Haitian society apart for the whole of its history. Yet the *Times* writer did not mention that Apaid, who pushed for Aristide's ouster, was white, or that the wretchedly poor people who created Apaid's wealth toiling for pittances in his sweatshops were black.

Incompetence alone would not explain an omission of such consequence. The wrongheaded description of the deteriorating social climate in Haiti had to have been intended. No journalist—certainly not one who lands a position at the *New York Times*—could be so blind as that.

In fact, Mr. Apaid is not Haitian at all but a white American citizen of Syrian extraction.

The vast majority of Americans, black and white, never knew that American policies were largely the cause of Haiti's political disintegration. Nor had they any idea of the extent to which those policies rendered positive change for Haiti's black poor, from the very first day of Haitian democracy, virtually impossible.

32

THE PRESIDENT'S WIFE SAT DOWN ON THE white damask sofa next to her husband. The airy living room was round and well-appointed but free of ostentation.

Fingering a book absently, he turned his head in her direction and said, "What time is it? We mustn't forget to call the children before they go to bed."

"In a few minutes—I spoke to them from the office this morning. Christine senses something. They want to know when they'll be coming home. Ordinarily they'd be fine with *Mèmère* (Grandma). But Christine senses that something is not normal. I'm not sure what or how much I should tell them."

"I know," he said softly. He rubbed his eyes again. They were quiet for a while. "We'll just have to take it a day at a time."

She rested her head on his shoulder. The tension flowed out of his body. By now they both knew that the Americans were behind all this—egging on the rebels, directing the opposition, calling the shots.

33

Tabarre, Haiti
Friday, February 27, 2004, 7:45 P.M.

T WAS FRIDAY, FEBRUARY 27, 2004, THE evening before the last day of Haitian democracy.

The setting sun angled its refracting rays across the round room and altered the color and feel of time winding down. Jean-Bertrand and Mildred Aristide sat hand in hand in the middle of the sofa in the middle of the room talking calmly and quietly to each other.

They were not afraid and did not have a moment's misgiving over the course they had chosen. Profoundly spiritual people, they held in their souls a trust that they believed would survive the looming tumult. Though their people were materially poor, the Aristides recognized and prized in them the storied heroism of the Haitian *nation* and the measureless contributions its stoop-laboring people had made toward preserving the African self in the West. Haiti was home to the last heartbeat of the Middle Passage survivors' dimming

141

memory of home. Ordinary Haitians believed this to be an ageless and immortal truth. They understood its price and were willing to pay it, while persevering to overcome those who had forced them to suffer for the crime of remembering themselves. If not in this life-time, then in the next, or the next after that. They knew who they were, who they had always been and who they would always be. They had time. They were *Haitian*.

Bits of ceramic, no matter how pretty and shiny, count for naught once they tumble from the mosaic's wedding. Similarly, the human story makes little sense when told in disassociated units of small mortal life, unrelated to a mothering culture that provides such life real and self-celebrating value—a place, one's own, to belong.

Haitians have a culture that slaves once bled to defend. Culture, when not crushed from without, can be virtually eternal. As can be the souls that shelter complete within its protecting arms. The result is a self-ownership, unfamiliar to me, that sets Haitians apart from those to the north and regions around, where wills and memories were broken, and souls were crushed in hot fields of cotton and cane. Haitians, having won their war, declined to ape the master as the rest of us, I suppose, had little choice but to do. To paraphrase Bob Mar-ley, they—the Haitians—more nearly than any of the rest of us *kept their culture*. For this, Haitians are reviled by a white world that the rest of us broken souls have long since succumbed to imitate.

34

Tabarre, Haiti
Saturday, February 28, 2004, 6:00 A.M.

A RELATIVE FEW AMERICANS KNEW WHAT wealthy white Haitians were doing to poor Haitians through their black surrogates in the years between 1957 and the coup of February 29, 2004. With the unpublicized support of the bourgeoisie, François (Papa Doc) Duvalier and his dreaded macoutes killed an estimated 50,000 poor blacks during his rule. His son, Jean-Claude, took up where his father left off. Even after Jean-Claude's expulsion from the country in February 1986, the slaughter of the pro-democracy black poor continued unabated. The American-armed military routinely rampaged through poor communities like Cite Soleil and Bel-Air, killing indiscriminately. In July 1987, the macoutes massacred three hundred small farmers who were protesting for democracy in Jean-Rabel. On September 11, 1988, the macoutes turned their guns on Aristide's packed church, mowing down twelve parishioners.

During the army coup against Aristide's first democratic government, 4,000 to 5,000 of the poor were killed. At least 4,000 more would be killed during the second coup, which was already under way. In the fall of 1991, during the run-up to the coup against the country's first democracy, wealthy families raised millions of dollars to pay for the assault against the Aristide government. Any soldier willing to shoot into crowds of people would be paid $5,000.

Everyone in Haiti knew that the wealthy white families, from the beginning, were working closely with the military to quash the new democracy and restore the military dictatorship behind which the rich, over the years, had amassed unseemly fortunes on the backs of the black poor. The powerful superrich families—the Mevs, the Bigios, the Boulos, the Apaids, the Nadals—enjoyed the full support of the United States.

From 1991 to 1994, large numbers of Haitians were killed by the reestablished military dictatorship. Many, but not all, of the victims were pro-democracy activists.

Conditions in Haiti were every bit as bad as they had ever been in South Africa under apartheid. But few in America knew this. And even those who did appeared not to know much about the mechanics of Haiti's oppression.

During President Aristide's three-year exile following the first coup against democracy financed by the bourgeoisie, two members of the Mev familiy came to talk to me in Washington. The meeting was arranged by Greg Craig, the Mev family's Washington representative. Craig was a successful lawyer, a liberal Democrat, and former staffer for Senator Edward Kennedy. Eight years before, I had worked closely with Craig and Senator Kennedy to win passage in the Senate of the Anti-Apartheid Act of 1986. I was shocked to find him in the pay of the Mevs who were, in my view, as guilty of crimes against humanity as South Africa's white supremacists had once been.

Owing to a scourge of American public ignorance, the Haitian bourgeoisie received a free ride from the American public, as did influential Americans like Craig who agreed to work for the bourgeoisie.

From the start, Aristide tried to establish an authentic democracy that could put a dent in the country's wide socioeconomic divide. From the start, the United States, France, the European Union, the Haitian bourgeosie, the macoutes, FRAPH, Convergence, and the American-armed rebels employed every imaginable tactic to violently defeat the new democracy's overarching goal.

In November 2000, Aristide was reelected for a second term as president with 90 percent of the vote. In elections held in May 2000, his party, Famni Lavalas, swept the national and local elections with 75 percent of the vote. Immediately Aristide's local and foreign enemies criticized him for not including in his cabinet the badly defeated candidate the electorate had roundly rejected. Against American and EU insistence, Aristide formed the government the Haitian electorate had voted for, a democratic, mass-based government. Aristide's foes wanted a "consensus" government that would include the losing parties that were hostile to Fanmi Lavalas's central objective, and that very few Haitians had voted for. The Bush administration and EU members continued to pressure Aristide to disregard the electorate and do what none of them would have done in their own countries.

Writes British author Peter Hallward, "No doubt *bona fide* democrats like Margaret Thatcher and Tony Blair have often been criticized, but perhaps rarely for their failure to include parliamentary opponents in their own cabinets."

In 2003, no one could remember an occasion where the United States and its allies had mounted a more comprehensive campaign to cripple a small, poor country than they had in the case of democratic Haiti. No stone was left unturmed. The United States sponsored the antigovernment radio stations that spewed antidemocratic propaganda around the clock. It sponsored rallies that called for the fall of the democratic government and the establishment of a parallel government of the U.S.-backed Convergence. During the reorganization and training of the national police following Aristide's return from exile in October 1994, the CIA interference was blatant enough to cause the U.S. Department of Justice official assigned to oversee the training program to resign in frustration in 1999. It was during this period that Guy Philippe, the Delmas police captain, was selected by the CIA for training in Ecuador and was later induced to commit treason against his country.

Aristide dismantled a vicious Haitian army that had killed tens of thousands of the poor, only to be left with a national police force that had been penetrated and compromised by the CIA.

By the fall of 2003, the United States and its local proxies had closed in on the government from all sides. The U.S.-imposed embargo had cut the government's budget in half. American-sponsored antigovernment radio programming and rallies were proliferating. The national police force was poorly equipped, ill-trained, and compromised. Former FRAPH operatives, Duvalieristes, and cashiered army thugs were training with American arms in the Dominican Republic and had already struck across the border into Haiti several times.

The British Nobel Prize–winning dramatist Harold Pinter got it right in explaining how Washington destabilizes countries from within: "It means that you can infect the heart of the country that can establish a malignant growth and watch the gangrene bloom."

In a stunning inversion of cause and effect, the Bush administration, taking lines from the theater of the absurd, *accused* Aristide and his democratic government of *defending* itself.

Aristide responded by saying that he "recognize[d] that institutionalized violence [against the government] is stronger than any we could unleash. We are not armed. And I do not believe that we will ever have the means to compete with the enemy on that key terrain. But they cannot count on me to condemn acts of despair or of legitimate defense by the victims of aggression."

Some of the "victims" in the early 1990s had formed themselves into groups of sparsely armed street children that Convergence, through the U.S.-sponsored Haitian media, later took to calling "chimeres" or "chimès," the name of a mythical fire-breathing monster.

In time, the government's foes, at least for foreign consumption, would successfully demonize the street children, and Aristide as well, by association, even though no connection between him and the "chimès" was ever demonstrated.

Douglas Perlitz had worked with such children in Cap-Haïtien for years. Commenting on their response to the turmoil of 1991, Perlitz said:

> The way I see it, it's as if the poor had been suffocated for decades, in fact for centuries; the rich and their army were like a hand keeping their heads under water, and they couldn't breathe. Aristide was the person who removed that hand. But when the people could finally lift their heads from out of the water, they didn't just gasp for breath, they also tried to lash out at the hand that had oppressed them for so long. Some popular violence in the wake of Aristide's election victory in 1990 was inevitable.

Gandhi himself would have been powerless to stop it. What's remarkable is that things never got out of hand. Under the circumstances, the level of discipline in the popular movement was very impressive.

The president's small book-lined office gave onto the living room and was adjoined on the roadside of the house by a security command post that was shared by Haitian Presidential Security and the Steele Foundation.

It was Saturday, February 28, Haiti's last day of democracy. At 6:00 A.M., the president entered his office through the door off the living room and sat down to read the morning papers. There were four of them. One was a local French-language paper and three were foreign—two French and an English-language daily from Jamaica called the *Gleaner*. The foreign papers were a day old. He read the local paper first and then the others.

Putting the newspapers aside, he reached for a report written by Dr. Yves Polynice, a Haitian surgeon who was dean of the Université Populaire, the medical school that his government had established in August 2001 for Haitian students possessing aptitude but lacking means. Classes had begun for a few students that year in November in a building at Lafanmi Selavi. Now there were 247 students and 30 professors at the university and the affiliated Hôpital de la Paix (Hospital of Peace), which was located at 33 Delmas. One of the professors was Dr. Paul Farmer of the Harvard Medical School. The new campus was inaugurated on November 14, 2003.

Little did the president know that by the end of the following week, the street children would be turned out of Lafanmi Selavi and the building shuttered. The 247 medical students enrolled at Université Populaire would be tossed off campus, their dreams of becoming doctors dashed. Invading American soldiers would claim and occupy the new medical school building, which had been built to advance the healing arts.

The president tried to work through a stack of documents but could not concentrate, something he had always been able to do quite effortlessly.

During his two broken terms in office, he and his government, and importantly his wife, Mildred, despite fierce opposition, had made noteworthy progress on Lavalas's social agenda. He now saw that progress disappearing like footprints in sand. It depressed him. Few outside Haiti knew anything about what they had tried so hard to do. The intense opposition from America and France obscured everything but the picture drawn of him by his enemies. Haiti's military dictators had been ridiculed in America, but he had been rendered virtually unrecognizable.

He questioned whether the source of this unfamiliar despondence was ego or the sight of his country's functioning new institutions pulled down around him. The Americans seemed to have the power to control perceptions of reality, if not reality itself.

America had not swayed the Haitian public, of course, but that had counted for nothing with the Americans. His government, retaking its place in 1994 from a military dictatorship that America had armed (and continued to arm), had begun its work when in 1991 the country had thirty-four public high schools for 8 million citizens. Now in February 2004 the country had 138, but what had this mattered to the Americans? They never seemed to be interested in such things. He had always believed good to be an irrepressible force from a higher plane that could prevail over naked power. But

the Americans, he supposed, would have thought such to be non-
sense, Christians though they ostentatiously presented themselves to
be. The truth was that while he knew how to stand up and speak for
the poor, he had come to doubt the influence of moral suasion on
those who valued only wealth and power.

But what could he have done differently? He had dissolved the
brutal army and he had never second-guessed himself for doing so. It
was the lethal creature of the old dictatorship, inherently disloyal to
democratic ideals and untrustworthy. In any case, what could the
army have been used for, except to war against the people they were
supposed to defend? As it turned out they had reconstituted themselves into a paramilitary force and terrorized the Haitian people
anyway, with American help.

The truth was, without power, he had no idea of how to fight
against those who had overwhelming power and respected little, if
anything, else.

He questioned whether he should have taken down the barriers.
No negotiations materialized from his concession, and the Americans must have known that none would. It seemed obvious now that
negotiations were never intended.

He looked through the door and saw his wife picking up the telephone in the living room. He watched after her for a while and pon-
dered how remarkable she was. She might easily have become one of
the countless acquisitive American careerists, safe and secure in a
Manhattan high-rise law career, but she'd walked away from that
without a moment's consideration to risk everything. Still, her resolve
remained the equal of his.

35

Tabarre, Haiti
Saturday, February 28, 2004, 7:00 A.M.

THE PRESIDENT WAS LOOKING AT, BUT NOT seeing, a picture on the wall opposite his desk. He was waiting without knowing what he was waiting for. Things had spun badly out of control. He thought back over the past two years and came up with little that he might have done differently. The "flawed" national elections of 2000 had given pretext, if not pulse, to those who opposed him and had already made up their minds to circumvent the constitutional order. *Seventy-five hundred* local and national seats had been contested in the elections. The outcome of seven of the contests, which were for Senate seats, had been called into question. The president persuaded the seven winners who were Lavalas members to resign the seats, and called for new elections, which the Bush administration and the International Republican Institute and its local creation, Convergence, spurned. The president had even offered to share power with the *unelected* opposition, but nothing he did would satisfy either the opposition or Washington, save his resignation and departure from Haiti. Notwithstanding his enemies' public statements, he had known from the beginning of his second term that they would stop at nothing to pry him from office.

"He wasn't going to be beholden to the United States, and so he was going to be trouble," Senator Christopher J. Dodd of Connecticut, a Democrat, would later say. "We had interests and ties with some of the very strong financial interests in the country, and Aristide was threatening them."

Beneath statues of Haiti's Revolutionary heroes, President and First Lady Aristide pay respects with Prime Minister Yvon Neptune on November 17, 2003, the 200th anniversary of the Battle of Vertierres. The battle, fought at a fort near Cap Haitien in northern Haiti, triumphantly capped Haiti's 13-year war against France, ending slavery in Haiti and sounding the death knell of slavery throughout the Americas.

Foreground (L-R): Prime Minister Perry Christie of the Bahamas, President Jean-Bertrand Aristide, and President Thabo Mbeki of South Africa release doves at Haiti's Bicentennial celebration on January 1, 2004. In the background are First Ladies Zanele Mbeki and Mildred Aristide.

A crowd of over 500,000 celebrating Haiti's 200th birthday stretch from the grounds of the National Palace to the streets beyond on January 1, 2004. Lydia Polgreen of the *New York Times* wrote that the crowd was "small, but enthusiastic."

Hundreds of thousands celebrate President Aristide's
inauguration of a public park in Delmas on February 7,
2004, three weeks before his abduction.

President Aristide and officials of his government serve
breakfast to Haiti's poor at the National Palace.

Paul Farmer, Harvard
Medical School professor and
a founding faculty member of
Haiti's new medical school
Université Populaire.

Haitians protesting against the Bush Administration's blocking of loans already approved by the Inter-American Development Bank for safe drinking water, education, and healthcare in Haiti.

Andy Apaid, American-born, wealthy leader of Group of 184—an unelected organization that helped to engineer the ouster of President Aristide and some 7,500 elected officials from office, as well as the president's ouster from his country.

On Saturday, February 7, 2004, three weeks before the dismantlement of Haiti's democracy, more than one million marched in Port-au-Prince demanding that Aristide be allowed to complete the five-year term to which he had been elected. The demonstration was largely ignored by the international media.

Homeless and "Restavek" children gather for weekly lunch and play at the Aristide family home in Tabarre.

On Constitution Day, President Aristide presents to police officers copies of Haiti's democratic Constitution and explains the importance of adhering to it.

President Aristide in December 1993 with Congressional Black Caucus Chairman Kweisi Mfume, Operation Push Chairman Reverend Jesse Jackson and the author. Black American support for Haitian democracy never reached the groundswell levels of support that it reached for South African democracy. In the rear to the author's left is seated Rene Preval who was elected Haiti's President after the coup d'état of February 29, 2004.

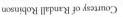

Courtesy of Randall Robinson

Guy Philippe, leader of the American-armed paramilitary force that terrorized the people of northern Haiti in the weeks leading up to the February 29, 2004, ouster of Haiti's government.

Emmanuel "Toto" Constant, founder of the Haitian death squad FRAPH, at a press conference in Port-au-Prince on September 16, 1993.

Frantz Gabriel, President Aristide's helicopter pilot, served in Vietnam as a sergeant in the United States Army's 11th Calvary Black Horse Division. He was an eyewitness to the abduction of President Aristide and his wife by American soldiers.

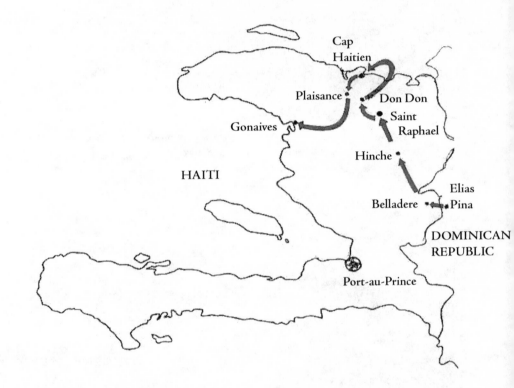

The northerly path that the American-armed paramilitary force followed from its base in the Dominican Republic, going away from Port-au-Prince before stopping near Gonaïves where the rebels remained.

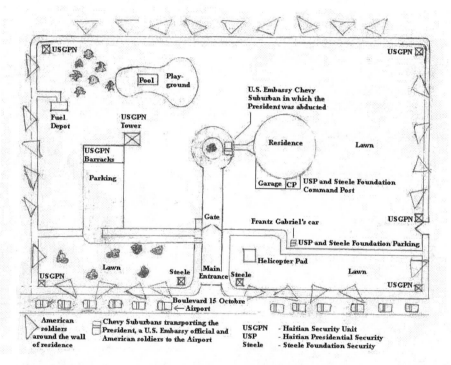

President's Residence at Tabarre, February 28, 2004, 4:00 am.

Two Customs Declaration forms (one for arrival and one for departure) filed in Antigua by the American Operators of the large white unmarked aircraft on which the Aristides were abducted from Haiti. The first handwritten arrival form falsely claims the flight to have originated in Guantanamo Bay. The second typed departure form shows the plane to have been carrying fifty passengers before the handwritten number was altered to "NIL" or zero. The form also shows the next intermediate refueling stop to be Ascension Island, a British and American military refueling station in the South Atlantic near the African continent. The form indicates that the plane left Antigua at 10:00 in the morning on February 29, 2004.

On the seventeen-hour overnight flight to Bangui, Central African Republic, Congresswoman Maxine Waters, the author, Sharon Hay-Webster, Ambassador Sidney Williams and Ira Kurzban plan a strategy to secure the release of President and Mrs. Aristide.

Mrs. Aristide and the author greet each other at the Presidential Palace in Bangui, Central African Republic, on Sunday evening, March 14, 2004. Behind the author are delegation members Ira Kurzban and Ambassador Sidney Williams. Standing in the right foreground is Frantz Gabriel, President Aristide's pilot and eyewitness to the President's abduction.

Mrs. Aristide and President Aristide waiting with the group from the United States and Jamaica to meet with President François Bozize to petition for their release.

President Aristide and his wife, Mildred Aristide, with President Bozize, having no way of knowing, when this picture was taken, whether the Central African Republic military dictator would ever release them.

President Bozize giving the decision to
the Aristides following his consultation
with Washington and Paris. To the left
are Congresswoman Maxine Waters and
Parliamentarian Sharon Hay-Webster
(partially obscured).

President Bozize releases the Aristides.
In the background are the author,
Sharon Hay-Webster and Ambassador
Sidney Williams (partially obscured).

Minutes before midnight, relieved but
drained, the author, Congresswoman
Maxine Waters, President Aristide and
Ambassador Sidney Williams walk
from the terminal toward the plane.

March 15, 2004

Dearest Hazel,

For some reason, our communication channel to you through Amy's operation in New York has gone down. We don't know why. In any case, I hope the problem is a temporary one. If it is not, I will have to wait until we reach Barbados to call you on Maxine's cell phone. Under the circumstances, however, I thought the wisest course would be to write this letter to you now. I will entrust it to someone at the airport in Senegal to mail from there.

Before her signal went down, the indefatigable Amy broadcasted, I think from Bangui, what we have been able accomplish. I am not sure that you have heard yet, but we were able to secure the release of Mildred and Titid. They are with us now on board with Franty Gabriel, the President's helicopter pilot. They, of course, are very tired, but are otherwise in sound health.

It is I am here. We took off from Bangui an hour ago. I do not know that "they" will allow us to get away with this. So long as we are over land, I feel relatively safe.

A portion of the letter written on the plane by the author to his wife, Hazel Ross-Robinson, shortly after leaving the Central African Republic.

President and Mrs. Aristide en route from Bangui to our first fueling stop in Dakar, Senegal.

President and Mrs. Aristide being welcomed to Jamaica by Jamaican Senator Delano Franklyn. Also pictured are the author and Sharon Hay-Webster (standing between President Aristide and Mrs. Aristide).

Amy Goodman of Democracy Now.

James B. Foley, the United States Ambassador to Haiti at the time of the coup d'état.

Governor Jeb Bush of Florida.

American soldier levels his weapon at unarmed Haitian male displaying five fingers of each hand—the nationwide signal demanding that President Aristide be allowed to serve the five-year term to which he was elected.

The author with President Jean-Bertrand Aristide in Pretoria, South Africa, October 2005.

36

THE INTERNATIONAL REPUBLICAN INSTITUTE
(IRI) is a nonprofit organization funded by the American
government and headquartered in Washington, D.C. It operates in
over sixty countries, ostensibly to help build mechanisms for democracy. Though it claims to be nonpartisan, it is commonly accepted
that the practices, policies, and decisions of the International Republican Institute are the practices, policies, and decisions of the Bush
administration, if not of President George W. Bush himself.

The leader of the International Republican Institute in Haiti was
Stanley Lucas, an implacable right-wing opponent of Aristide and a
black. A wealthy Haitian stalwart of the cabal dedicated to the overthrow of the democratic government, Lucas, as early as 2002, impor-
tuned the opposition that IRI had created, to refuse negotiations
with Aristide's democratically elected government: "Hang tough.
Don't compromise. In the end, we'll get rid of Aristide," he had
urged.

Jean-Max Bellerive, a prominent Haitian bureaucrat who had served in three governments, including Aristide's, said of Lucas, "He said there was a big plan for Haiti that came from Washington, that Aristide would not finish his mandate." Bellerive said further that Lucas told him that the American ambassador to Haiti, then Brian Dean Curran, who had begun to recognize the antidemocracy thrust of Haiti's monied interests, "was of no importance, that he (Curran) did not fit in the big picture."

Two years after the coup d'état, the *New York Times* reported:

> With Washington's approval, Mr. Lucas used (American) taxpayers money to fly hundreds of opposition members— but no one from Aristide's Lavalas party—to a hotel in the Dominican Republic for political training that began in late 2002. Two leaders of the armed rebellion [Guy Philippe and Paul Arcelin] told *The Times* that they were in the same hotel during some of those meetings, but did not attend.

Lucas, the IRI senior program officer and scion of a wealthy Duvalierist family, appeared on February 8, 2001, on Radio Tropicale in Haiti and proposed a number of strategies for ending the democracy led by Aristide: (1) jailing the president on corruption charges and (2) arranging to have the president meet the fate that Congolese President Laurent Kabila had met in Kinshasa a month before.

Lucas, who spoke with greater authority for the Bush administration than did the American ambassador to Haiti, asked over public airways, "You did see what happened to Kabila?"

Kabila had just been murdered by an assassin.

Neither President Aristide nor his wife, Mildred, had ever seen Stanley Lucas, and had no idea of what he looked like.

In July 2004, five months after the coup d'état, Max Blumenthal, an American, wrote:

> The role of figures like Lucas in the coup suggests a complex web of Republican connections to Aristide's ouster that may never be known. What is clear, though, is that the destabilization of Aristide's government was initiated early on by IRI, a group of right-wing congressmen and their staffers, by imposing draconian sanctions, training Aristide's opponents and encouraging them in their intransigence. The Bush Administration appears to have gone along, delegating Haiti policy to right-wing underlings like the assistant secretary for the Western Hemisphere, Roger Noriega, a former staffer to Senator Jesse Helms, Republican–North Carolina. Not only did Noriega collaborate with IRI to increase funding to Aristide's opponents, but as a mediator to Haiti's political crisis, he appears to have routinely acquiesced with the opposition's divisive tactics.

Blumenthal's observation falls somewhat shy of the mark. With its $3 million per annum opposition-organizing program in Haiti, the IRI, for all intents and purposes, *was* the opposition to democracy in Haiti.

37

Tabarre, Haiti
Saturday, February 28, 2004, 7:45 A.M.

T HE PRESIDENT SAT AT HIS DESK ALONE WITH
his thoughts. He was essentially a contemplative man, and reserved by nature. Thus the depth of his anguish could not easily be
gauged. Despite the pressure on him, he appeared outwardly calm, as
if he knew the things that needed to be known, or was it perhaps that
he saw, but not quite literally, the things that needed to be seen. Or
maybe, nearer to the heart of it, he *believed* in the things he needed to
believe in. His life—the voice he had given to the *invisible ones*—the
sureness with which he gave that voice, all seemed to have been fashioned around a central life-justifying idea—a call, wrought from the
world's holiest books, for a certain nonnegotiable restitution to the
wretchedly poor—the long-ignored afflicted, whose indelible psy-
chic pain he knew to be indistinguishable from his own—the long-
suffering mothers, the worked-to-an-early-death fathers, their

mothers, their fathers. Eight million black *peyizans* were bound to-gether by an abusive experience rooted in Haiti's slave history.

He had been called some of everything by the foreigners who saw life and the world only *their* way—flat, unremembering, and in the present tense—the Americans, the French, the Canadians—for the most part who found no place for cosmic or spiritual curiosity, had no time or appetite for factual investigation—egoistic people from egoistic cultures who knew nothing about the Haitian heart, the Haitian way of thinking, the pathos that informed it; people—crisp-talking, object-oriented, get-to-the-point people who did not know him or anything about him.

The foreigners had power, and that covered it. They would never put themselves on trial for anything and no one else could. That was the nub of it.

Dean Curran, the American ambassador, whom many Americans saw as a good guy, a decent white American type, a better than the Republican smash-mouth ideologue type but pretty much blind like the rest—Curran had said of the president (quite paternalistically, I should mention) that "in the end, he (meaning the President) disap-pointed me."

Should anything of consequence turn on such a wrong-end-up vertical remark from a mere ambassador about a head of state—a re-mark that, one could argue, describes the unexamined bias of many, if not, most Americans toward a large slice of humanity?

Max Blumenthal, a liberal teller of considerable American stature, wrote, "To be sure, Aristide was a corrupt, problematic leader."

The president lived faithfully with his wife, who was also his best friend, and his two young, well-reared daughters in a pleasant, modest house. His tastes were quiet—not ascetic, but toward that direction.

His appetites for food and drink were abstemious. Never had he or his wife displayed any signs of wealth. Save their home, they were not known to own anything. No one could sustain a claim that they had any money or property besides the house, which has since been looted and vandalized. Powerful nations have combed every data-bank in every country of the world for evidence of stashed assets and found nothing.

Serious American writers do not carelessly describe the president of the United States as "corrupt." Were they to, they'd be driven quickly from the ranks of serious American writers. White writers, when writing about American and western European political fig-ures, take pains to get their facts straight. They do this, of course, for ethical reasons, but, more importantly, they do it to preserve their sinecures in the prestigious club of lettered American know-it-alls.

For those writing about African or Caribbean heads of state, the rules are different. Claims are not vetted, no matter how specious or unproven they appear on their face. Like Mr. Blumenthal, American writers are free to say, loosey-goosey, any unsubstantiated thing that arrives in their heads about the world's black leaders. They suffer no career penalty at all for the reckless saying of it.

As for the matter of Aristide being a "problematic leader," I would guess that this is what the "disappointed" Ambassador Curran may have been alluding to. From an American vantage point, the claim may well have been quite square to the mark.

In my view, at least, Aristide was never a politician. (Many years ago, before I met Aristide, Michael Manley, the prime minister of Ja-maica, by way of introduction said to me of Aristide, and only half jokingly, "You know he's a bit of a mystic.") And I doubt that he ever really tried to turn himself into a politician. With all the trade-offs, the diplomatic gobbledygook, the self-emasculating forbearance, the numbing ceremonies of do-nothingism, my guess is that he had had little aptitude or tolerance for the sort of wheel-spinning exertions that bring one full circle with no tangible result.

He was the leader in his country of a groundbreaking social cause—a cause he saw to be, in its essential ethic, moral. That he was not a politician annoyed the Americans who desired to manage and manipulate him. It was, however, that same visionary and relentless quality of self-possession that endeared him to the Haitian poor who had elected him president twice, and would have done so again, given a chance.

The president's important enemies were the wealthy and powerful, inside and outside of Haiti. If the president had a price, as Blumenthal seems to suggest, and that price was money, the powerful interests that came to regard him as a formidable threat would never have needed to coproduce his ouster. What maddened his rapacious local enemies, as well as the United States, was the jarring fact that the president of Haiti was anything but an ambitious, self-seeking, rigmarole-spouting politician who could be "talked to" and ultimately bought off. Without realizing it, Blumenthal concedes the point by allowing that Aristide was "problematic."

For whom?

Certainly not Haiti's ill-treated black poor, who saw in the figure of their president a chance to complete the realization of Toussaint L'Ouverture's dream for his people. It was for *them* that L'Ouverture and hundreds of thousands of slave revolutionaries had triumphantly created the republic.

Having attempted and failed to compromise him, Aristide's enemies—the United States, France, Canada, and other European countries; wealthy white and self-defined nonblack Haitians; and power-hungry unelectable black Haitians—slandered Haiti's democratically elected president as "insane," "dictatorial," "tyrannical," and "corrupt." Senator Jesse Helms, the Republican chairman of the Senate Foreign Relations Committee, even called him, on the floor of the U.S. Senate, a "psychopath."

The man—caught recourseless and defenseless in the American crosshairs, isolated under the hot glass reticle of America's high-powered global disinformation gun—a president of a country, who opened schools and clinics for the poor, who brought new and real hope to millions, who opened his home on Fridays, without fail, to scores of homeless and poverty-stricken children—a man such as this, who, though little known to Americans, was seen as a hero by the vast majority of his people. A man like this was being called by American officials, diplomats, politicians, writers, spies, and local barbers everything but a child of God. The tellers had loosed the lemmings. Their coup, having already begun, had become by then a fait accompli.

The president and his wife endured what was said about him (and about her as well) with great dignity. By Friday, the day before the coup, Hazel and I had not seen them for months, and had to take our readings from the timbral quality of their voices over the telephone. She spoke somewhat faster than he, but that had always been so. His temperament appeared as even as ever, and he remained unfailingly solicitous and gracious, as if he were impervious to the vicious stories swirling about him.

38

Paris, France
Thursday, February 26, 2004

ON FEBRUARY 26, TWO DAYS BEFORE ARIS-
tide's disappearance, the French foreign minister, Dominique de Villepin, blamed Aristide publicly for the spreading
violence and called for a "new government of transition" that would
exclude him. Beyond the moral and constitutional absurdity of such
a declaration, had Villepin any higher right to demand Aristide's resignation than Aristide had to demand Villepin's? Did Haiti's hard-
fought independence count for nothing within the family of nations?

The old-timers of my childhood admonished an overreacher with
the rebuke: *Know your place!* The trouble was, insofar as the black
world was concerned, the white powers of the world believed that
every place was their place.

On Saturday, February 7, 2004, three weeks before the coup, a million Haitians marched in Port-au-Prince to demand that the president

be allowed to finish his five-year term to which he had been elected. The marchers separated their five fingers and thrust them into the air to represent the five years of his term. The demonstration had no effect. The international press ignored it, as well as others like it that were just as large, while covering every smallish public effort undertaken by the wealthy foes of Haitian democracy.

The president had to feel worn down by the building weight of all this. For months he had leaned over backward to reach a workable accommodation with the United States, Group 184, Convergence, and the rebels. He felt the only genuinely democratic path out of the impasse to be new internationally monitored elections. Such a course was anathema to Group 184 and Convergence, however, since neither group had a prayer of winning a fairly run democratic election. Still, Aristide, with considerable misgivings, agreed to negotiate a solution. He even accepted a set of proposals from Group 184, only to see his acceptance rejected by the proposal's architects. He was then presented with a new set of even more onerous conditions, one following after another—a series of them pressed on him in accelerating waves of bad faith.

Luigi Einaudi, the Organization of American States (OAS) representative, had led the democratic government on a fruitless wild goose chase from the very start of the crisis. Willingly doing the bidding of the United States and Haiti's powerful business class, Enaudi and Group 184 piled condition atop condition, making it shamelessly clear in the end that their sole objective was the democratic government's unconditional ouster.

Within the OAS, only the Caricom countries consistently attempted to defend the democratically elected government. But those governments wilted under American pressure and accepted the opposition's oxymoronic premise that an endangered *democracy* could be salvaged via an *undemocratic settlement*. A month before Aristide's disappearance, Jamaican Prime Minister P.J. Patterson, chairman of Caricom, threatened to "impose sanctions on Aristide" if he did not cooperate.* Kofi Annan, secretary-general of the United Nations, behaved with equivalent spinelessness, doing and saying nothing worthy of recall.

---

* I published a letter to Prime Minister Patterson in several Caribbean newspapers questioning the wisdom of his and the general Caribbean's flaccidity. I warned them that what the United States was doing to one small Caribbean nation, on this occasion, Haiti, it might just as easily elect to do to them all at a later date.

39

Tabarre, Haiti
Saturday, February 28, 2004, 8:00 A.M.

THE PRESIDENT BROKE FROM HIS RUMINATION and looked again at his wife who was talking on the telephone in the living room. He could not hear what she was saying. Then she gave a small laugh. It raised his spirits and sent him imagining whom she might be talking to. He guessed somewhat absently that she might be speaking to the ninety-year-old mother of Micheline Dalencourt, Christine's and Michaëlle's piano teacher. The mother was a mulatto woman of French and African descent. She lived with her daughter, Micheline, in an aging wooden gingerbread house in Bois Verna, a faded former haven of the Haitian bourgeoisie. Mildred Aristide would have called the piano teacher, but only as a courtesy. Surely Micheline Dalencourt already knew that there'd be no lessons, at least for a while.

In normal times, on Thursday afternoons, the First Lady would sit on the front gallery of the house and talk to the elderly mother while Christine and Michaëlle played for their teacher in the parlor. The old woman, plucky and clear of mind, would speak nostalgically of her youth growing up in the old house and of the year 1915, when Woodrow Wilson ordered soldiers into Haiti. She talked of how the Americans had all but destroyed the country, killing thousands and stealing everything that was worth anything. She recalled to the First Lady what the marines had done to Charlemagne Peralte, the peasant farmer who had tried with his Cacos (revolutionary peasants) to resist the marines.

The marines killed the thirty-two-year-old Peralte and nailed his corpse, crucifixion style, to a piece of wood for public display. This was done to teach a lesson to any who were contemplating further resistance.

For the old woman, time seemed to have stopped there, fixed in place like the hands of her old Benrus beneath its age-clouded crystal. She was three years old when the marines marched into her country. She was twenty-two when they left. Vivid girlhood images of the lumbering English-speaking killers haunted her reveries still. She spoke of this often to the First Lady on piano Thursdays while sitting on the gallery of the crumbling memory-filled family home in Bois Verna. Her recollections of that long and wrenching time now prefigured and intensified for her the terror that America was yet again ushering into her country's national life.

40

Tabarre, Haiti
Saturday, February 28, 2004, 11:15 A.M.

N THE LATE MORNING OF SATURDAY, FEBRUARY 28, Hazel and I reached the president and his wife by telephone for the last time. They first asked after our daughter, Khalea, who was fourteen. They wanted to know how she liked her school and how she was doing in Third Form.* We talked at some length about that, and then about how Christine and Michaëlle were doing in Miami. They said that the girls were doing well, given the circumstances. There was nothing otherwise remarkable about what they said or what we, in retrospect, might have inferred from their language. We ended by talking about Tavis Smiley, who would be interviewing the president on the next day, Sunday, at the National Palace.

---

* Third Form is the equivalent of the freshman year in an American high school.

That night Hazel and I lay awake worrying about what calamity might have befallen our friends, suddenly cut off from the entire outside world, whom we could neither reach nor find.

It was dark in our bedroom and quiet, save for the sharp song of crickets and the soft round bump of waves lapping soothingly against the black volcanic rocks in the surf below our bedroom window. We lay on our backs watching the ceiling fan turn lazily beneath its shadow.

We had been quiet for a while.

"Hazel," my voice whispery against the room's darkness.

"Yes."

"Are you still awake?"

"Yes."

"I've never talked to them about their faith. Have you?"

"I spoke to him once when he was in exile in Washington. On 7th Street."

"Was he still a priest?"

"I can't remember. I think so. . . "

"What did you talk about?"

"I asked him what God was."

"What did he say?"

"He was very human and nonpreachy. He said, 'First of all, God is love. That means that wherever there is love, *true* love, with kindness and compassion and honor and respect, God will be there. And God's goodness and mercy will be there. At the same time, God is all around us, and more importantly, within us. And so, each time you observe an act of kindness, an act of compassion and consideration, an act of mercy or justice, no matter how large, no matter how small, *that* is a manifestation of God. These are all manifestations of the

God within us—proof of the divine spark that is within us all. And acts of kindness and mercy all around the world combine to create the Goodness and Mercy that *is* God—on a much larger and more dramatic scale."

41

THE PEOPLE—DISPROPORTIONATELY AMERI-
cans—who run much of the world have a built-in advantage
over those who would quarrel with their decisionmaking. American
public officials often do not speak in plain, transparent terms about
what all they are doing. They are even less candid about *why* they are
doing whatever it is that they may be doing or laying plans to do. The
few Americans who look behind their leaders' delusive public pro-
nouncements get to see but a fraction of their decisions and actions
before those decisions and actions produce benefits and consequences for the millions, at home and abroad, who are affected by
them.

With democracies and dictatorships alike, the real, determining
factors in policymaking are largely unknown to the various affected
publics. They are as little known as the identities of the policies' real
intended beneficiaries, and are as little known as the decisionmakers

who burrow about anonymously in the bureaucratic machinery of meddlesome governments.

In the case of Haiti, the American public was allowed to see little of the looming coup d'état long in the making. Even when the American public was given a glimpse of the elements of the coup, it had no way to interpret intelligently what it was looking at. If ever there was social tumult that appeared from televised images to be the making of black people alone, the February 29 coup in Haiti was it. For perhaps the first time in modern diplomatic history, blacks appeared to be in charge of everything.

After all, Haiti was a black country with a black president and a black government. To a man, all of the rebels endeavoring to overthrow the black president and his black government were black as well. In short, virtually all of the people who *appeared* to be involved, or at least those shown as involved to Americans on television, were black, including the American secretary of state, the American president's national security adviser, and the secretary-general of the United Nations.

This conveniently picturesque conflux of blacks, some well-placed, most not, served the interests of the real U.S. decisionmakers and the Haitian white and mulatto business class—the intended local beneficiaries of the coup—quite well indeed. For if you are going to overthrow a black democracy, let black people do it, or at least *appear* to do it. It goes down better everywhere that way—especially with blacks, judging from the reaction I got from blacks I knew, who were thinly informed about what was actually going on in Haiti.

It was against this meticulously falsified backdrop that those of us—blacks and whites—who fought the coup's American planners were made to appear hopelessly quixotic.

In the U.S. Congress, Representative Maxine Waters must often have seemed so. But she did not allow herself to be put off course by how she was likely being perceived.

42

Los Angeles, California
Sunday, February 29, 2006, 1:20 P.M. PST

"WHAT IN THE WORLD HAVE THEY DONE WITH them?" Waters asked worryingly on the telephone to Hazel and me.

We had no idea.

"Did you see what the networks did?" Hazel asked in an incredulous tone.

"You mean the airport footage?"

The American television networks had been airing old footage shot in natural light at the Port-au-Prince airport showing President Aristide without his wife, shaking hands and making his way along a line of government ministers before boarding a nearby commercial aircraft. The networks represented the footage to be pictures of the president's *voluntary* departure from Haiti. The three of us knew immediately that the claim could not possibly be right. The film that the networks aired was shot in natural light. The president had departed the country with his wife in the early hours of February 29. The plane in the film had commercial markings. We already had learned from witnesses at the airport in Antigua that the president and his wife were likely aboard a large white aircraft with an unmarked fuselage. We would later learn that there were no cameras at the airport to record the president's departure from Haiti. Nor were any officials of his government present.

Why did the networks air footage they knew to be a misrepresentation of the truth? Had Bush administration officials asked them to use the misleading footage in an attempt to corroborate the administration's claim that President Aristide had "fled" Haiti? If the president's departure had indeed been voluntary, why had there been no news network television crews at the airport to film his departure when they had been filming every second of the "uprising" up until then, as had been the case previously when *unelected* Haitian dictators were chased out of the country under American protection?

Save for a comparative few (e.g., Marguerite Laurent, a Haitian American lawyer and president of the Haitian Lawyers Leadership Network, Amy Goodman of Democracy Now, and Kevin Pina, a correspondent for *Black Commentator*) who were able to look behind the incomplete, if not wholly erroneous, accounts that world mass media were giving to various publics, only a discerning handful of people had such questions occur to them. As a result, the vast majority of Americans accepted the Bush administration's story that President Aristide and his wife had "fled" what Times Online of the United Kingdom was still calling "a popular revolt" as recently as February 2006.

The Bush administration knew that when it came to Haiti, which was commonly perceived to be uniformly black and poor, it could do virtually anything that it wished, without political or strategic consequences. In the eyes of the administration, no one *who counted* would suffer in Haiti, and no one *who counted* would care in the United States. Black Haitian democrats had no force of friends in America who mattered to the Republican president or to the U.S. Congress.

Colin Powell, the secretary of state, and Condoleezza Rice, the national security adviser, were among the most respected people in America. More importantly, they were black. If *they* didn't care about what was happening to Haiti's democracy, why would an archly conservative white American president, at whose small-minded pleasure they relished to serve, care? After all, the machinations of the two of them together were largely the reason what was happening to Haiti was indeed happening.

In fairness, and for sake of perspective, it is important to note that Americans generally did not care—Democrats, Independents, Republicans. In fact, Americans ascribe importance to *no* black country, whether democratic or not. For them, Haiti's problems were anything but surprising, to say the least. America had long been an unreflective racist social organism with an appetite for the timely provision of fodder. Black, dysfunctional Haiti had long been a favorite American fodder selection. African Americans, scarcely better informed than white Americans about Haiti and the world generally, had little choice but to interpret the Haitian crisis as yet another mildly embarrassing outcome of black-on-black folly, to which they responded by covering their eyes.

●　●　●

It was early Sunday afternoon on February 29. Less than twenty-four hours earlier, Ron Dellums had reported to Hazel that Colin Powell had told him the rebels would be coming on Sunday to kill President Aristide, and that the United States would do nothing to protect him. Raising the hue and cry with journalists, we had tried as best we could to protect him. Now he and his wife had vanished.

I put the telephone down to get the door. Hazel continued talking with Waters.

"What happened between Randall and Ron?" asked the congress-woman. "I spoke to him this morning. I've never seen him like that."

Hazel was mystified. She was not aware that anything had happened between me and Dellums.

"He was very upset that Randall told journalists to call *him* to verify what Powell had said to him."

I was astonished when later told of this. Like Hazel, the former congressman worked as a lobbyist for the democratic government of Haiti, whose president, Jean-Bertrand Aristide, according to Colin Powell, would be assassinated by American-armed rebels sometime on Sunday, February 29. According to Dellums, Powell had further said that he, or rather the United States, would do nothing to prevent the killing. Tavis Smiley had told Hazel that Dellums had also told him this. I was surprised to learn that Dellums would be upset with *me* for doing what I thought he himself might have been doing independently. Inasmuch as I knew with certainty that Aristide would not voluntarily leave Haiti—not even to save his own life—many of us who were supportive of Haiti's democracy felt a heavy responsibility to do everything possible to protect the life of the country's twice-elected president, and that included shining the brightest media spotlight possible on the rebels' assassination plan that Powell had divulged to Ron Dellums.

Hazel, years before, had worked with Dellums when he was chairman of the House Armed Services Committee. They had a relationship based on shared politics and mutual respect. After Dellums retired from Congress, Hazel persuaded President Aristide to hire him as a lobbyist for the government of Haiti. In the month that followed the Sunday telephone conversation with Maxine Waters, Hazel placed three calls to her old friend and colleague. He did not return them. Neither Hazel nor I have spoken with him since.

43

Basseterre, St. Kitts
Monday, March 1, 2004, 11:15 A.M. EST

A S IF TO HERALD THE MOMENT'S WEIGHT, THE line hissed and cracked for what seemed an eternity. Slowly, out of the noise materialized the far-off sound of the president's voice. "Randall . . ." his voice swimming in and out, "Randall . . ."

"Yes," I answered loudly.

"This is Titid."

"Mr. President, where are you?"

"We're in the Central African Republic. They brought us to the Central African Republic . . ." the voice fading, then strengthening, "It was a coup. Tell them for us it was a coup . . ." The connection died.

44

Elias Pinas, Dominican Republic, rebel base camp
Monday, February 2, 2004

T HE MEN HAD BEEN WAITING SEVERAL DAYS for their orders, although they would not see or know for certain who would give them. All the same, they sensed that they would be moving soon. The weather had been hot and dry. The River Massacre, ten meters wide beside the little Dominican village of Elias Pinas, had shriveled up and cracked into a parched arroyo. The two-hundred-man force would have to cross over to Belladere on the Haitian side of the dry riverbed before the rains came.

Men about to enter combat speak sparingly if at all, and only when required. These men did not behave in the usual way. They had been told that they would soon be overthrowing the government in Port-au-Prince. They appeared jubilant about the prospect and were eager to get on with it. None of them, as it happened, expected to be facing real combat conditions. After all, they were heavily armed with new

American weapons and ammo. The few police brave enough to contest then had no way to answer their firepower. The rebels, outfitted smartly in baggy camouflage with bulletproof vests and steel helmets, had good reason to expect that the mere sight of them would scare the bejesus out of lightly armed policemen defending a lightly staffed police post, miles and mountains distant from Port-au-Prince, the capital.

The Haitian rebels waiting at the base camp near Elias Pinas had been trained by United States Special Forces. The rebels had appeared for their American training in the Dominican villages of Neiba, San Cristobal, San Isidro, Hatillo, and Haina. They had arrived for the sessions dressed in the uniforms of the Dominican Republic national police.

Today, poised to storm the defenseless peasant-populated countryside of northern Haiti, they wore the camouflage battle dress of their American benefactors. Over the past two years, the men had undertaken several full dress rehearsals that included the attacks on Haiti's National Palace and the Police Academy on Route de Frères. They had carried out still more destructive forays, once against a hydroelectric power plant and three times against police stations in the Central Plateau area of the country.

The Americans did not have to teach them how to kill. *This* they already knew how to do. The Americans had only to overlay the rebels' pulsating appetite for killing with a patina of military discipline.

Oiled M16 components lay on mats in the clearing where the rebels were meticulously cleaning what their American Special Forces operators had taught them to refer to as *weapons*, never guns or rifles or other such unprofessional terminology. The *weapon*, gleaming and oiled, was to be kept near the professional soldier at all times, they were told. The *weapon* was the professional soldier's killing machine, his dearest and most reliable friend.

A short, well-muscled rebel sitting on a mat with his legs akimbo pulled from the bore of his weapon an oiled patch of soft cotton that he had run with a long steel rod several times up and down the length of the bore. With his right eye, he painstakingly inspected the barrel for motes of dust. Satisfied, he carefully reassembled the state-of-the-art weapon that had been supplied to him by the United States via the army of the Dominican Republic. He cocked the M16 and pulled the trigger. The clean metallic clap of the weapon's action sounded sweet enough to provide him a small liquid thrill.

Many of the assembled killers readying themselves to raid the democratic republic across the river had once been members of the Haitian Armed Forces (FADH), the cashiered Haitian army that for many years supplied menace and muscle for the old Duvalierist dictatorships. Others of them had served in the Front for the Advancement and Progress of Haiti (FRAPH), the brutal paramilitary death squad that once terrorized the country as a night-riding adjunct to FADH. Human rights organizations reported that between the years 1991 and 1994, the night killers of FRAPH had massacred some five thousand Haitian civilians. Anyone with democratic sympathies qualified for their attention. In those days, they worked with knives, machetes, and chains. In the days ahead, they would use the American M16 automatic assault weapon.

Numeric values cannot express the horror and breadth of human rights atrocities. Numbers have no faces. Numbers trivialize the quality and miniaturize the scale of human suffering. Numbers are flat, numbing, impersonal. Human suffering is not. Human suffering can only be grasped one face at a time. Of the numberless dead and maimed FRAPH faces, I have only seen one in the flesh. Her name was Alerte Belance. I met her some years ago on the *Phil Donahue Show*. Harry Belafonte and actress Susan Sarandon were also on the show in support of Haiti's pro-democracy movement. Belance explained how a group of FRAPH thugs had descended in the night upon her home in Cité Soleil looking for her husband, who was suspected of "supporting democracy." Failing to find him at home, they turned their whistling machetes on young Mrs. Belance, cleanly severing an arm at the elbow and filleting her face free of her skull. Left for dead, she had miraculously survived by fleeing into the midnight sea.

One of the men responsible for what happened that night stood on the edge of the clearing in the Dominican Republic, dressed like the others in American issue, with one minor difference. Instead of a steel pot and helmet liner, he wore a fashionable soft camouflage bush cap that tied under his chin. He was a tall, fiftyish man with an Afro that bloomed neatly beneath the edge of his cap. A cigarette dangled cynically from the right corner of his mouth. He had the kind of dissolute good looks that habitually mistreated women find attractive. The eyes told unmistakably that Louis-Jodel Chamblain was a ruthless man. A cofounder of FRAPH, a Duvalerist military death squad leader, a convicted murderer; after the coup d'état, Amnesty International would call on United Nations peacekeepers to arrest Chamblain for his alleged involvement in a variety of war crimes committed in 1987, 1991, 1993, and 1994. The murder conviction was reached in absentia after Chamblain fled the country upon Aristide's return in 1994. Chamblain and others had been found responsible for the brutal killing of Antoine Izmery, a wealthy white supporter of democracy who had been dragged from church on Sunday morning and shot to death on the church steps in broad daylight.

Chamblain stood in the deep shade of a boxwood tree talking to Guy Philippe, the former Delmas district police chief. The two men, at least visually, presented a study in contrasts. If Chamblain had the countenance of a pitiless killer, Philippe cut quite a different figure. At thirty-five, he looked clean-cut and blameless. Few who knew him as a police chief would have imagined that he would one day be involved in a bloody putsch to overthrow a democratic government.

As a young policeman, he had performed his job competently enough. He was never known to abuse his power and had no early reputation for cruelty. When people were suspected of plots against the government, he willingly arrested them.

Things changed. His lifestyle suddenly outstripped the ability of an $800-a-month policeman to pay for it. Observers noted that he had begun mixing with the "wrong people," who presumably could help him afford the expensive clothes and fast cars the boyish-looking police chief had developed a taste for. Perhaps he developed a sympathy for the wealthy class that he now relished joining.

Setting himself apart from Aristide and his campaign to help the poor, Philippe spoke understandingly of the centuries-long tradition of the rich paying nothing into the public till and having public policy matters wholly their own way. He said admiringly that the wealthy "have maintained a stark class system in Haiti for two hundred years" while disdaining to appear the least bit critical of the wealthy's lethal selfishness: "They have a key role in this country."

With an emphasis that would leave little doubt in the minds of those Haitians he believed counted, he publicly announced that the man in the world he most admired was the former Chilean dictator General Augusto Pinochet, who "made Chile what it is."

Perhaps it would be naïve to accept that Philippe's basic character *deteriorated* over a span of a few years. It is more likely that he arrived, finally undisguised, as the person he had always been—a small-minded opportunist willing to do virtually *anything* to achieve personal ends, including murder and, finally, treason. These essential proclivities of his character must have been known to the United States as far back as the early 1990s, when he was plucked by the CIA out of a Haitian military regime for training in Ecuador by U.S. Special Forces.

Before fleeing to the Dominican Republic in October 2000, he was discovered to be plotting a coup d'état. Well before this happened, while he was still serving as the Delmas district police chief, the UN/OAS international civilian mission to Haiti learned that dozens of local gang members had been summarily executed by police officers serving under the command of Philippe's deputy, Inspector Berthony Bazile.

Three weeks after the coup, Philippe is said to have ordered Ti Gary, a paramilitary subordinate, to go and kill Lavalas party supporters in the poor neighborhood of La Savanne. When Ti Gary refused to comply, Philippe's deputy shot him.

●　　●　　●

Chamblain and Philippe move deeper into the lengthening shadow of the boxwood tree. Philippe says something that causes Chamblain to laugh. The men in the clearing who are cleaning their equipment steal a glance at their leaders.

By then, in every respect, these were America's men, her property, her agents, her rabble proxies. Not merely the two speaking quietly beside the clearing, but all two hundred of the men readying to cross the riverbed. To a man they were experienced criminals and not of the petty stripe. There they gathered in a remote glade by a border sitting on the raw ground preparing to lay waste to a poor black people's embryonic democracy—a motley amalgam of killers, drug runners, embezzlers, kleptocrats and sadists—joined only in their loathing of those who looked like them. They were prepared to murder thousands to bring down a democratic government in order to elevate themselves—and all this only for the barest impermanent measure of atavistic dim-witted power to inflict corporeal *pain*, and—God yes, embarrassingly—to achieve a small surreptitious notice from the very Americans who despised them all, traitor and democrat alike.

In general, it cannot be gainsaid that the country's elected parliamentary membership, in the year before the coup, was earnest, competent, and surprisingly well-educated, given all that Haitian society had endured. The American officials who met with members of parliament from time to time were loath to be seen in daylight with the sociopathic types they had armed to the teeth to overthrow the president and members of his parliament, and thousands of similarly elected officials along with them.

Indeed, the wealthy white and mixed-race elites, whose interests the rebels were lustily defending, and whose interests the Americans decidedly favored, were scarcely less morally culpable than the rebels themselves. Groups that the wealthy elites supported, and that unofficial organs of the U.S. government like the National Endowment for Democracy funded, had "even installed spy cameras in his [Aristide's] Presidential residence," wrote John Maxwell, the Jamaican writer, "and published a photograph of Aristide, naked, in his bathroom."

It was not as if American officials did not know whose blood-spattered bed they had crawled into. Indeed, they had made the bed.

By the time the United States had provided the rebels with three hundred or more M16s, ammo, uniforms, grenades, grenade launchers, M50s, bullet-proof vests, boots, helmets, and crates of general ordnance, the killers led by Chamblain, Philippe, and Francois Emmanuel "Toto" Constant had already slaughtered thousands of innocent civilians. Chamblain had long before been implicated in the 1994 Raboteau massacre.* Later, he and Constant would meet with an unidentified army officer on the morning of October 14 of that year to discuss plans to gun down the widely respected justice minister Guy Malary on a Port-au-Prince street.

If these armed putschists had had an ambassador to the United States, it would likely have been Emmanuel "Toto" Constant, who was, with Chamblain, a cofounder of FRAPH and a paid informant of the Central Intelligence Agency. Constant lived under unofficial American protection in Queens, New York, his paramilitary brainchild, FRAPH, killing, between 1991 and 1994, thousands of would-be Haitian democrats, maiming still more like Alerte Belance, and driving tenfold others like them fleeing into the Caribbean Sea.†

---

* On April 18 and 22, 1994, the Haitian army and FRAPH carried out a combined raid on scores of homes in Raboteau, a poor coastal community on the outskirts of Gonaïves. Hundreds were beaten and tortured. Up to a hundred defenseless people were killed. Among those convicted were Louis-Jodel Chamblain and Jean Pierre Baptist.

† On July 6, 2006, Francois Emmanuel "Toto" Constant was arrested in Riverhead, New York, by the Suffolk County Police Department on mortgage fraud charges. On October 24, 2006, while Constant was still being held on the mortgage fraud charges, Sidney Stein, a U.S. district judge sitting in Manhattan, found him "liable for torture, attempted extra-judicial killing and crimes against humanity." The judge ordered Constant to pay $19 million in damages to three Haitian women who claimed they had been gang-raped by FRAPH members under his command.

In Haiti's two-hundred-year history, one is hard put to identify a single episode of organized human suffering in which the United States did not play a direct, collateral, or instigative role. The story of the horrific death squad killings of FRAPH is no different. Toto Constant himself attributes FRAPH's founding to Colonel Patrick Collins, an officer of the United States Defense Intelligence Agency. According to Constant, Colonel Collins approached him following the first coup d'état that ousted Aristide in 1991 and persuaded him to organize the front that in August 1993 became FRAPH.

It is not known when Guy Philippe first boasted publicly that he would go to Port-au-Prince and kill Aristide on Philippe's birthday, February 29. Nor is it known why he made the boast. It is also not known that he, from the beginning, ever intended to carry though with his threat. We do know, however, as events were to unfold, that mounting a frontal attack on Port-au-Prince would have produced a massive bloodbath and an international public relations disaster for the United States, the country, acting alone, that had directly and indirectly (via the International Republican Institute), trained, armed, equipped, and likely commanded the rebels.

The rebels' task was to terrorize the countryside outside of Port-au-Prince—to hack, murder, burn, loot, raze—to tear a fiery swath of destruction across the northern half of Haiti. To create a televised spectacle of the swaggering killers' unimpeded march from town to town, taking studious heed to space their conquests so as to extend and maximize the news media's coverage of what appeared to be the inexorable fall of the democratic government, village by defenseless village.

It was to be a frightening, murderous, well-planned, well-disguised diversion on which all attention would be focused.

45

Elias Pinas, Dominican Republic
Early February 2004

EARLY IN THE FIRST WEEK OF FEBRUARY 2004, some two hundred well-armed rebels broke camp at Elias Pinas, Dominican Republic, boarded military vehicles, and moved slowly across the dry riverbed of the Massacre River and onto Haitian soil well north of Port-au-Prince. They would take the path of least resistance—west and then north *away from* Port-au-Prince—stopping first inside Haiti at Belladere, a small town from which most of the men left in the old days to serve in the long-disbanded Duvalierist army.

The force was nominally under the command of Guy Philippe and Louis-Jodel Chamblain, though the consensus opinion of the government in Port-au-Prince was that neither of the two was really in charge. More likely, the government thought, the shots were being called by the Americans who had armed, trained, and made them possible.

Of all their new weapons, the rebels were proudest of the M16s that had been delivered to them by the Dominican Republic from a lot of twenty thousand provided to Santo Domingo by Washington the year before. Santo Domingo had been more than happy to do Washington's bidding in this respect. Like Washington, the rebels, Convergence, and Group 184, the leaders of the Dominican Republic wanted to see the democratic government in Port-au-Prince toppled—and not just for reasons derived from its traditional racialist enmity toward Haitians of African descent. The policies of the Aristide government had begun to hurt a Dominican economy that relied on poorly paid Haitian migrant stoop labor to cut sugar cane. President Aristide, telling Haitians they would be better off staying at home, as opposed "to going over there," had jeopardized the Dominican Republic's supply of cheap field labor. Fewer and fewer Haitians were willing to work for the pittance offered across the border.

From Belladere, the rebels turned north to Hinche where they attacked a police station and gave chase to a policeman armed only with a .38 caliber pistol. The rebels released ten prisoners from the station lockup, looted the place, and then burned it to the ground.

Later, on February 22, Lydia Polgreen (the *New York Times* journalist who had described the bicentennial turnout of hundreds of thousands as "small but enthusiastic") would name Gonaïves as "the city where the uprising began on February 5." Polgreen would get the story wrong on two counts. What was unfolding in northern Haiti was not an "uprising" but a well-planned diversionary rampage of American-armed thugs, who, beginning with the little town of Hinche, were attacking lightly defended hamlets along a northerly course toward Cap-Haïtien and *away* from the capital.

The rebels' path was being tracked from the air by Frantz Gabriel, the pilot of the government's leased Huey helicopter, who reported it to Port-au-Prince. From Hinche, the rebels drove north to Saint Raphael, killing several unarmed civilians en route, where they burned the police station and received international media attention for the first time.

The rebels spent roughly two hours in each village before moving on to their next target. They would reach little Dondon on the second day of their drive north.

46

National Palace, Port-au-Prince, Haiti
Saturday, February 21, 2004, midmorning

REPRESENTATIVE MAXINE WATERS SAT IN THE
spacious meeting room next to her husband, Ambassador
Sidney Williams. The assemblage was larger than the two of them
had expected it to be, with five or six groups represented. The high
ceiling seemed to facilitate the hushed flight of whispered voices
from one end of the oblong chamber to the other.

Seated in the room were President and Mrs. Aristide along with
several members of the government.

The antigovernment Haitian groups present had been formed
into something called a Council of Wise Men, which was a recent or-
chestration of the Americans. Among its constituent factions were
Group 184, Convergence, and the local diocese of the Catholic
Church. Also present was a representative of the Organization of
American States.

Directly across from Waters and Williams sat two people with whom they had flown into Haiti from Miami, Fred Mitchell, the Bahamian foreign minister, and Roger Noriega, the American assistant secretary of state for Latin America and the Caribbean.

Were success to have a distinguishable visage, it might well have been Foreign Minister Mitchell's. Everything about him seemed to have been designed, constructed, and neatly placed with deliberation—his features, his build, his suit, his sunglasses, his gestures, his speech, his carefully controlled bearing. Assistant Secretary of State Noriega, seated next to him, suffered strikingly by comparison. The American was short and dumpy with nervous eyes that flitted erratically like the head of a small bird. His was the mien of one who'd been mocked and bullied through much of an unpleasant childhood and adolescence. This may or may not have had something to do with his thinly disguised dearth of sympathy for the poor, dark, and disadvantaged of the countries affected by his policy work.

To Water's surprise, Noriega and Mitchell had not come to ask the president to resign—at least not in so many words. The meeting itself had been all but forced on the president as American news coverage of the rebels tearing around in the north intensified.

Mitchell had already spoken twice in the meeting, describing to the president how things *were*, so to speak. When the foreign minister was not talking, he was listening to Colin Powell's representative, Roger Noriega, who'd been whispering into the Bahamian foreign minister's ear throughout the meeting.

Waters locked eyes with Mitchell, disturbing his pearlescent poise, but only for a moment. Up until that point, the Bahamian foreign minister and the American assistant secretary had tried and failed to have the congresswoman and her husband (who'd once been the American ambassador to the Bahamas) removed from the room.

Then someone midway down the table was describing to the twice-elected president an offer being made to him by the unelected Group 184. The speaker couched the proposal in daunting language as the president's last best chance. Under the proposal, the unelected Council of Wise Men, not the president, would select a new prime minister to run the country, although the president was the only person legally authorized to make such a designation under the Haitian constitution.

Waters continued to stare at Mitchell, while Noriega continued to whisper into Mitchell's ear.

At this point the president shocked the unelected Wise Men by accepting the proposal made by the unelected Group 184. Stunned and unable to accuse the president of obstinacy, Noriega requested a sidebar with the president in the president's office. The president left the meeting room with members of his government to join Noreiga and Mitchell in his office. Mrs. Aristide and several members of the government remained in the conference room with Waters and Williams.

The president returned to the conference room with Noriega and Mitchell to conclude the meeting. With a smile, he praised Waters's presence and invited her to speak before making his closing remarks.

From the beginning, Convergence, the brainchild of the International Republican Institute, and Group 184, the front for wealthy businesspeople who paid negligible wages and even less in taxation, had wanted the president ousted from the country. They had not expected him to accept their proposal.

Now Group 184 found itself in the embarrassing position of having to reject the president's acceptance of its own offer. This, however, is precisely what the American-supported members of Group 184 did.

● ● ●

The army of paramilitary killers rolled into Dondon and repeated its performance in Hinche and Saint Raphael. They shot the few policemen who showed themselves, released all prisoners from jail, and burned the police station to the ground.

International camera crews in trucks now trailed behind the rebels as they rumbled overland with their mounted M50 machine guns blazing, from one hapless settlement to the next. Meeting only sporadic resistance from lightly armed rural policemen, the rebels appeared to have been having fun. The now familiar scene of petrified hillside villagers engulfed by noise, fire, and death resembled a movie set more than a battleground.

Given the northward course of the rebels, it was becoming increasingly apparent that their real goal was not to overrun the capital far to the south (from which the barricades would soon be cleared at the request of American officials), but to terrify the north—and gain misleading notice for it.

From Dondon with news media in tow, the rebels set their sights on Cap-Haïtien, the country's second largest city, with 500,000 residents, located on the north coast. There the rebels would meet with something more than token resistance. The fighting took place in the vicinity of the airport, where police tried to defend the city with .38 caliber pistols and a few shotguns. The brave but ill-advised effort cost the police force more than thirty lives.

Following a pattern established in the towns they had overrun on their way north to the sea, the rebels again cleared the jail of prisoners and torched the building before throwing open the port's warehouse doors and inviting looters to cart away pilfered goods.

Of the city's half million residents, fewer than one hundred came out onto the streets to welcome the rebels, who set up headquarters at the Mont Joli Hotel. Television footage showed Guy Philippe bent Pattonesque over a long map table set up before a bank of running news cameras. In the harsh white glare of the television lights, he was declaring his arrival, surveying the mapped domains of his now undisguised ambition, playing loosely for the cameras the increasingly important role of himself. It was cinema vérité—murderer-cum-general-cum-president style. Adrenaline surges seemed to render him temporarily delusional. He had given himself over to a real belief that he *would* become president of Haiti.

He was America's tool and therefore America's responsibility. It was the United States that chose and egged on the corrupt, half-educated young man who would later be discarded as an embarrassment, not only by Haitian voters in the February 2006 elections but also by the United States that had trained and used him in its plot to rid Haiti of its democratically elected president.

But for now, the world's cameras were trained on Philippe. He could not have known at the time that those moments at the map table in Cap-Haïtien on the Sunday afternoon of February 22, 2004, would mark the apex of his public career.

Because it selects and circumscribes, television overstates the importance of everything it presents. Anyone watching the television coverage of the rapidly unfolding events in Haiti would have thought the entire countryside had been set ablaze by the rebels. Those outside of Haiti could only assume that the rebels would capture Port-au-Prince in a matter of days, if not hours.

I was very worried. I called the president's home at Tabarre and spoke to Mrs. Aristide. She reassured me that while events in the north were disturbing, the rebels posed no threat to the government. She seemed certain that they would not risk coming to Port-au-Prince. I had trouble reconciling her equanimity with the alarming pictures on television. I didn't know the country's rural geography and could not see that the rebels had been turning noisily in a slow circle.

While Philippe pored over his maps on that Sunday afternoon in Cap-Haïtien, Paulda Petime, a twenty-three-year-old member of Philippe's force, was telling the *New York Times* that the rebels would take Port-au-Prince within twenty-four hours, or sometime on Monday, February 23. Philippe had promised to kill Aristide no later than February 29, Philippe's birthday. Colin Powell had given Philippe's boast credence with his telephone call to Ron Dellums, asking him to convey to Aristide two important pieces of information: Philippe was coming to kill the president on Sunday, February 29, and the United States would do nothing to protect him.

The president and his wife remained in Port-au-Prince throughout the week of February 22, making plans for the Sunday interviews at the National Palace with Tavis Smiley and George Stephanopoulous.

Instead of moving on to Port-au-Prince as Paulda Petime had promised the *New York Times*, the rebels left Cap-Haïtien and drove south to the tiny riverside hamlet of Plaisance (Pleasant Place), where they repeated the crimes they committed in Hinche, Saint Raphael, Dondon, and Cap-Haïtien. They then drove south to Go-naïves and stopped.

Port-au-Prince is a two-hour drive south from Gonaïves along a coastal road. When President Aristide and his wife disappeared during the early hours of Sunday, February 29, 2004, Guy Philippe, Luis-Jodel Chamblain, and their American-armed paramilitary force were in the vicinity of Gonaïves, one hundred kilometers north of the capital, presumably awaiting further instructions.

During the rebels' winding rampage of homicidal terror through the north, the nearest they came to Port-au-Prince was Belladere, their first stop after crossing the border from their training camp at Elias Pinas in the Dominican Republic.

Colin Powell's attempt to frighten Aristide into abdicating his constitutional presidency had not worked. By then it had become plain enough that Philippe and the rebels were never coming to Port-au-Prince, which Powell would almost certainly have known when he spoke to Dellums.

Not only were the rebels never coming to Port-au-Prince, circumstances would soon dispositively show that they had never even been rebels. They were, as things turned out, little more than willing (and very likely unwitting) decoys whose roles in a murderous plot ended hours, if not days, before the coup and Aristide's disappearance.

47

Pétion-Ville, Haiti
Sunday, February 29, 2004, 3:15 A.M. EST

N THE LATE AFTERNOON OF SATURDAY, FEBRUARY
28, the president's helicopter pilot, Frantz Gabriel, reported for
the last time to the government on the pattern of movement and exact whereabouts of the American-armed paramilitary force that had
ground to a full stop somewhere in the neighborhood of Gonaïves on
the northwest coast of the country.

Gabriel believed that the "thugs were afraid to come into Port-au-
Prince" and said as much to his superiors in the government. Unlike
most Americans who did not know what Haitian town or city was
where, Gabriel had good reason to believe that while Philippe,
Chamblain, and their followers had caused great damage in the
north, they did not pose a serious threat to the government.

Gabriel had lived in America and served as a sergeant in the
United States Army. As a consequence, he knew who Tavis Smiley

was and went to bed in his Pétion-Ville home on the evening of February 28 with the idea of driving into the National Palace on Sunday to see Smiley's interview with the president.

The telephone rang in Gabriel's home at 3:15 in the morning. The call was made by one of the president's Haitian security guards who said to Gabriel in Kreyol that "there is something happening that I don't understand. I think you'd better come here." The voice on the phone had been colored with alarm. Gabriel dressed quickly and went out, positioning on the front seat of his car beside him an M3, the equivalent of a small M16 automatic rifle. The streets would be deserted at this time of night, and Gabriel expected to reach the president's home at Tabarre in twenty minutes.

* * *

Besides the president, his wife, and the few Haitian security personnel present at the president's home in the early hours of February 29, Frantz Gabriel would be the only eyewitness to the coup d'état and abduction of the president and his wife that was carried out between 3:45 and 4:00 A.M. by American Special Forces soldiers.

On October 25, 2005, I took this statement from Gabriel in Pretoria, South Africa, where he was living in exile.

> I got to the house at 3:30 A.M. on Sunday morning. The gate is usually opened by a member of the CAT team (Haitian Counter Ambush Team). That morning it was opened by the Steele people. This never happened before. (I later thought that the Steele people had gotten a call to play the game, to play along.)

The gate closed behind me. I parked in my usual space in the parking lot on the right between the two walls. I left the M3 on the seat of my car. I walked through the second gate and into the command post. No one said anything to me. I then walked through the office and then into the president's living room.

The president was standing alone in the room dressed in a suit with a white shirt and a dark tie. The First Lady was somewhere else. She was not in the living room.

I then asked, "Is there a problem, Mr. President?"

The president said, "There has been a lot of pressure coming from all different directions."

I said, "What do you mean, sir?"

He said, "The way things are looking—I am under intense pressure."

The phone rang and the president went to answer it. I heard him talk. No American forces were there at that time. While he was on the phone, I said to myself that I should go out and see what was going on in the yard where Haitian security and the Steele people were.

As I walk out [the front door], pulling up to the walk to the front door is a big white Suburban with diplomatic plates. I was standing by the steps to the door. [Luis] Moreno gets out of the Suburban with two American soldiers. I turned and went back into the living room to be closer to the president. The president is putting the phone down.

Moreno said, "Mr. President, I'm from the U.S. embassy. Ten years ago, I was there when you came in. I was there to greet you. It's too bad that ten years later, I'm the one that has to announce to you that you've got to go."

I look at the president and then at Moreno. By then the First Lady had come downstairs. The president went into the dining room to speak with her. They came out together. The First Lady was carrying a small bag. She was wearing a suit.

Outside there were twenty to thirty American soldiers on the walls that surrounded the house. They had lasers on their guns that made red dots. The red dots filled the yard. They were crisscrossing and coming from all directions.

The two soldiers with Moreno were Special Forces. I knew this because they had beards. They carried M16s and wore full battle dress with steel helmets and bulletproof vests. They were white and said nothing.

We got into the Suburban. The president sat in the second row by the window. The First Lady sat in the middle and Moreno sat by the sliding door. The two soldiers sat up front with one of them driving. I sat in the back row.

We went through the main gate and made the right toward the airport. Outside the gate, we were joined by a convoy of ten U.S. embassy vehicles. They were all white Suburbans. We made a right into the airport in the direction of the general aviation area. There were two hangers there. The old Huey helicopter was there. There was a white Airbus there. It had a huge American flag on the tail. There was no tail number and no other markings.

Moreno opened the door and got out of the Suburban. He said to the president and the First Lady, "Okay, let's go."

That's all he said. He didn't say anything to me. He stood at the foot of the plane and sort of motioned to the president, the First Lady, and me to board the plane. The three of us went up the stairs into the plane. The two American soldiers who were in the Suburban boarded the plane and changed into civilian clothes (polo shirts and sneakers) while the door was still open.

Moreno never boarded the plane. The [American] ambassador was not there.

All this happened very quickly. Everything was timed so well. The Suburban came into the yard at about 4:00 A.M. We got to the plane at about 4:30 A.M. The Suburban went right to the bottom of the stairs. We sat in the Suburban about five minutes before Moreno opened the door and said, "Okay, let's go."

The plane looked like it would seat about 365 people. All the window shades were pulled down. Behind the first seating section was a big operations center with telephone, a fax machine, and a computer. The machines were on one side of the plane and there were seats on the other side.

The president and the First Lady were told to sit in the front seating section. I sat ten rows behind a bulkhead that was behind the American soldiers who were behind the operations center. I could not see the president and the First Lady from where I was sitting, but I went to talk to them several times. He was quiet. She was crying silently. I said to myself, This is incredible. This is a kidnapping. They just came and kidnapped the president in his home and took him away. I'm in the middle of a fucking kidnapping. This is the first thing that hit my mind.

There were about thirty American soldiers on the plane. They came from the house in the ten Suburbans. They all had beards. They boarded the plane with their gear and then changed into civilian clothes. One of them, who seemed to be in charge, said to me, "Are you going back with us?" like he thinks I am one of his men. Maybe it was just because of my beard.

The American soldiers sat on the plane between me and the president and the First Lady. All the way in the back behind me were the Steele men with their wives and children. They were all wearing casual clothes. The pilots wore regular pilot's uniforms. We waited on the plane about thirty minutes before we took off.

There were five black people on the plane. Besides the president, the First Lady, and me, there was a Haitian woman who was with one of the Steele men. They had a baby. After we landed the first time, I asked somebody where we were but nobody would tell me. Everybody was quiet. I heard the fuel nozzle attach. Once in a while the baby would cry. After the baby was fed, everything was quiet again. They offered the president and the First Lady some sandwiches, but they did not take them.

We were on the ground for five hours. The guys who spoke to me before, who seemed to be in charge, said to everyone over the PA system, "So far we don't have an official invitation yet for President Aristide. It seems like nobody wants him." The guy was on the phone the whole time behind the president who was sitting face forward. His staff was also on the phone. Some of the phones were black and some were red. They were using the fax and the laptops also.

We flew for a long time after we took off again. We landed again and waited on the ground for fuel. We didn't know where we were. When we were approaching the Central African Republic, the guy who was in charge asked me, "What are you gonna do? Are you going back with us?" I told him that I was staying with the president. Then he said, "You are going to a French military prison." This is what said to me. I said, "I don't care, I'm going where the president goes." Then he said, "You will be greeted by a French colonel on your arrival."

No Americans got off the plane. Nobody. Only the three of us. Only the Central African Republic minister of foreign affairs came on the plane. We left the airport before the plane took off. Before that, we went into a small terminal. It was in the morning. We sat in the terminal for thirty minutes. The minister allowed journalists to ask him questions, but he was in no mood to talk. Then they drove us to President Bozize's palace. The president was out of town. They took us to two rooms in a side section of the palace. It was three days before President Bozize returned from out of town.

You asked me if the Central African Republic people were respectful to us.

The only time that they were a little disrespectful was when your plane came.

It was later that day on Monday, March 1, after the president had reached the Central African Republic, that he called me and announced, "It was a coup."

Aristide told the world press, which by then had migrated in numbers to Bangui, that American soldiers had forced him from his residence. "They came at night. . . . There were too many. I couldn't count them."

By that time, the United States had long since begun claiming publicly that Aristide had left Haiti of his own free will. Secretary of State Colin Powell in Washington called Aristide's claim that he had been abducted "absurd. . . He was not kidnapped. We did not force him onto the airplane. He went onto the airplane willingly, and that's the truth." The facts, however, do not support Powell's claim.

First, the president had no reason to "flee" Haiti as Powell and the media in general claimed he had done. The American-armed paramilitary force had not advanced beyond Gonaïves and showed no signs of moving farther south. Moreover, all the evidence showed a decisive disinclination on the part of Guy Philippe and Luis-Jodel Chamblain to try and take a capital of more than a million largely hostile residents with a force that scarcely numbered two hundred. Philippe and his men were a smokescreen, not a serious army. The president and First Lady were so confident that they had little to fear from Philippe and Chamblain that they spent Saturday evening at home in Tabarre *outside* the capital, and not in the National Palace at the well-buffered center of Port-au-Prince. Only a few days before, the Aristides had graciously, but firmly, turned down an offer for evacuation assistance from Representative Barbara Lee of the Congressional Black Caucus, and proceeded energetically about the task of finishing arrangements for the two television interviews scheduled at the National Palace midday on Sunday.

Two days after the coup and a day after the Aristide arrival in Bangui:

> [President] Bush telephoned French President Jacques Chirac on Tuesday to praise "the excellent French-American cooperation in Haiti" and "to thank France for its action," said Chirac's spokeswoman Catherine Colonna.
>
> Chirac told Bush he was "delighted by the quality of the cooperation" between the two countries in handling the Haitian crisis and the relatively smooth departure of Aristide. But there was no comment from the French Presidential palace of whether that cooperation may or may not have extended to forcing Aristide to leave.
>
> *MSNBC.com*

When the American aircraft carrying the Aristides to the Central African Republic landed for refueling at what we would later learn was Antigua, Antiguan officials who were friends of ours reported seeing an aircraft fitting the description given by Frantz Gabriel sitting for five hours with its shades drawn in a remote spot on the airport tarmac. Antiguan officials were not allowed to follow the normal procedure of boarding the plane. Information on the customs declaration aroused suspicion that something was amiss. Inside the plane, Mrs. Aristide attempted to raise the shade and was told by the American soldier who appeared to be in charge that she was not allowed to do that. She then asked where they were and was told by the soldier that he was not authorized to tell her where they were or where they were going.

If the president were "fleeing" to safety as the Americans insisted, why hadn't he been taken to nearby Jamaica, where Prime Minister

Patterson was willing to grant him asylum, as opposed to having him dragooned to an undisclosed destination halfway around the world? Why would the president, as the Americans were claiming, choose to go to the Central African Republic, a nominally independent military dictatorship that was, for all intents and purposes, controlled by France, a country, along with the United States, that had long sought Aristide's ouster from Haiti?

Further strengthening this point, in a telephone conference call after the coup involving Representatives Charles Rangel, John Conyers, Maxine Waters, and myself, Prime Minister P.J. Patterson told us that National Security Adviser Condoleezza Rice had directly threatened Jamaica for offering asylum to the Aristides. If any harm were to come to a single American soldier in Haiti, Rice warned Patterson, Jamaica would be held directly responsible, simply for allowing Aristide to remain in the Caribbean region. The United States wanted Aristide not only out of Haiti but out of the Caribbean. Halfway around the world, in the Central African Republic under American and French control, was about as far away from the region as they could take him.

The United States behaved very differently toward the Haitian military dictators who were forced from power in 1994 after overthrowing Haiti's first democratic government in 1991.

The dictators—General Raoul Cédras, Colonel Roger Biambi, and Police Chief Michel François—were flown out of Haiti (before an audience of television and print journalists) on an American aircraft to nearby Panama, where the three men continue to live comfortably.

After they departed, their homes in Haiti were guarded by U.S. soldiers at U.S. taxpayer expense. General Cedras's home was even rented by the U.S. government, thereby ensuring a continued flow of U.S. taxpayer dollars to the military dictator whose soldiers had been armed by the United States. The general himself had been trained at the School of the Americas.

Michel François was later indicted by the U.S. Justice Department for shipping cocaine valued in the millions of dollars from Haiti to the United States. Extradition to the United States for trial was arranged but then blocked on "national security" grounds. François remains free, living, like Cedras and Biambi, within an hour's flying time of Port-au-Prince, without objection from the United States.

No pictures or film exist of the Aristides being taken from their home by American soldiers under cover of darkness. No pictures or film exists of them boarding the U.S. aircraft that took them eight thousand miles away to a landlocked African military dictatorship under the sway of France.

Why?

Had the United States asked any one of the eleven English-speaking Caribbean democracies to offer the Aristides asylum, the invitation would have been accepted as a matter of course. Given the coup's provenance, however, the United States was not of a mind to do such a thing. Jamaica, to its enduring credit, would have to extend its offer of temporary asylum over strong opposition from the United States.

●   ●   ●

The red laser dots were gone. The walls around the empty house were now clear of American soldiers. Save for the small clicking sound of the palm fronds that rose and fell gently on the tropical night's warm breath, all was perfectly still at Tabarre with the exception of the building's open front door creaking slowly to and fro on its hinge. The virtually soundless American operation had raised no alarm in the surrounding neighborhood. Anyone walking along Boulevard Octobre 15 could have sauntered through the two road-side gates and into the large yard unbothered.

Lamplight shone out of the house's open front door and onto the short foot path that led to the circle where the white Suburban had come to a stop in front of the house minutes before. From the circle, the living room furnishings could easily be made out. There was the white damask sofa situated between tables bearing two burning lamps that emitted a soft yellow light. The room appeared to have been exhaustively searched by the American invaders. The more common breed of vandals would have to wait until daybreak for their go at things. During the hours that separated the two assaults, the room seemed to wait quietly. *Investir dans humain* was gone from its accustomed place on the coffee table. The China and flatware remained in a cabinet in the adjacent dining room to the left. Upstairs, closets still housed all the family's clothes, save those that the Aristides were wearing when they were taken away.

No preparation of any sort had been allowed by the foreign invaders. This caused the well-lighted rooms to appear as if the occupants had gone out for a short walk in the walled yard.

On a sideboard in the dining room stood seven or more family pictures angled back against their stands. Most of the pictures were 5x7s. The two 8x10s stood at the opposite ends of the sideboard. These were recent snaps of Christine and Michaëlle concentrating over a piano keyboard.

In each of the round house's rooms, family pictures, memorabilia, and creature comforts of a related sort—school art, school projects and reports, children's books, a clock-radio, the president's safety razor—could be found in plain view. Nothing seemed to have been touched or retrieved or taken away.

This did not seem to be the home of people planning on leaving it for good.

•   •   •

On Friday, February 27, at 11:16 P.M., the evening before the coup began, Mildred Aristide sent two e-mails to Hazel. The messages were answers to e-mails from Hazel about the interviews scheduled on Sunday, February 29, with Tavis Smiley. Hazel's e-mails would later disappear from her computer:

> From: Mildred Trouillot
> Sent: Friday, February 27, 2004 11:16 PM
> To: Hazel Ross-Robinson
> Subject: Re: IMPORTANT MESSAGE FROM TAVIS
>   SMILEY
>
> Hazel,
> I'll check with JB [Jean-Bertrand], but I think that it is definitely doable [Tavis Smiley interview]. He is about to make a statement on the State TV calling for calm, asking for the thugs to drop their guns, etc. This is in response to a US embassy communiqué asking for the "rebels" to retreat and for the population to "stop looting." It's late I will call first thing in the morning with the answer for Tavis. Is that Tom Joyner the DJ??
> Mildred

Hazel then sent another e-mail, as adviser to the government, checking on the George Stephanopoulous interview, also scheduled for Sunday, February 29.

From: Mildred Trouillot
Sent: Friday, February 27, 2004 11:17 PM
To: Hazel Ross-Robinson
Subject: Re:

Yes, the Sunday morning show. Someone did call. We have
to work out the logistics. Will the interview be videotaped, or
just audio? I'm not sure.
Mildred

On Saturday, February 28, beginning at 10:09 in the morning,
Mildred Aristide sent Hazel three additional e-mails, the first and
last of them to Hazel alone, and the second to Hazel and to Dr. Paul
Farmer of Harvard Medical School and Université Populaire. The
last e-mail was sent at 3:49 P.M. in the afternoon, just hours before
outside telephone access to the Aristide home was severed and President Aristide and his American-born wife were abducted from their
home by American forces. The message makes reference to work that
Mrs. Aristide, Hazel, and I were doing to complete the arrangements
for Tavis Smiley's interview that was scheduled for the next day, Sunday February 29, at the National Palace:

From: Mildred Trouillot
Sent: Saturday, February 28, 2004 10:09 AM
To: Hazel Ross-Robinson
Subject: Re:

I will call you in a little while.
Mildred

From: Mildred Trouillot
Sent: Saturday, February 28, 2004 11:04 AM
To: PEFARMER@BICS.BWH.HARVARD.EDU
Cc: hrr@rosro.com
Subject: Haiti

Paul and Hazel,

What can we do with this:

On February 7, 1993 Sen. Kerry issued a statement on the 2nd anniversary of JBA's inauguration, he criticized international efforts to return President Aristide as "too weak, too late, too low-level and too poorly enforced. This is not an issue that has two sides. If what has happened in Haiti over the past year is not wrong, then nothing is wrong."

Mildred

From: Mildred Trouillot
Sent: Saturday, February 28, 2004 3:49 PM
To: Hazel Ross-Robinson
Subject: Re: Haiti

Hazel,

I have since spoken to Randall. Am still waiting for the info on Tavis' flight. Let me know.

Thanks,

Mildred

As further evidence that President Aristide and his wife, Mildred, were not planning on Saturday, February 28, to leave the country, Michelle Karshan, the president's foreign press liaison who spoke with him several times a day, e-mailed to Hazel at 6:31 P.M. on Saturday a business-as-usual statement from the president describing a two-hour radio call-in show he had appeared on the night before from 11:30 P.M. until 1:30 A.M. Saturday morning.

On the show, he had admonished the public. "If you think barricades are necessary, yes, you can do that. But when the sun appears and people have to go to work, the barricades must be moved so cars and people can get on with their lives and people can go to work. . . . I will also be in my office on Monday." He then urged the "terrorists" to stop the killing. "When terrorists kill, we all suffer."

The day after President Aristide and his wife were taken from their home, Guy Philippe, the leader of the American-armed paramilitary force, appeared on television. When asked where he was, he said that he was "hours away from Port-au-Prince." The inadvertent admission (largely overlooked by the international media) further strengthened the president's claim that he and his wife had not left Haiti voluntarily on February 29—indeed that they had had no reason to leave but were forced out by American forces and not by the thugs who were "hours away" in Gonaïves *before, during,* and *after* the coup d'état.

Officials of the Bush administration and members of the Republican-controlled Congress took no pains to disguise their satisfaction with the involuntary departure of President Aristide from Haiti. Among the most ardent Republican opponents of the Aristide government had been Republican congressman Mark Foley of Florida, who all but gloated over Aristide's removal from Haiti: "He was either leaving on a Learjet or in a casket."*

* In the fall of 2006, Foley was forced to resign from Congress following televised reports from ABC News that he had sent e-mails that were sexual in content to underage boys serving as congressional pages.

While leading congressional Democrats did not assign Haiti's crisis the highest priority, they did take strong issue with their Republican colleagues over what actually had transpired in Haiti.

Two and a half weeks after the coup, Democratic Senator Christopher Dodd of Connecticut, citing U.S. Defense Department letters indicating that the United States had supplied 20,000 M16s in the recent past to the Dominican Republic, asked Assistant Secretary Roger Noriega if the guns had ended up in the hands of Guy Philippe and Louis-Jodel Chamblain. Noriega denied that the guns had ever been delivered to the Dominican Republic, though the senator had paperwork to show that they had indeed been delivered. "The question is: Was the Dominican Republic being used as a staging ground for weapons transfer and coup plotting?" remarked a Dodd aide.

The U.S. Senate might have scheduled a hearing to answer a more important question: Was it American forces who carried out the coup d'état against the democratically elected Haitian government while U.S.-armed paramilitaries were bivouacked in Gonaïves two hours north of Port-au-Prince?

Homing in on this, the most germane of many questions surrounding the coup, Jamaican Prime Minister P.J. Patterson and the leaders of the other Caribbean democracies called for a comprehensive investigation of the events of February 29. Caribbean heads of state also warned within days of Aristide's abduction that what had happened to their democratic colleague signaled a "dangerous precedent for democratically elected governments everywhere." Sue M. Cobb, the American ambassador to Jamaica, rankled many in the Caribbean by countering that the response to the Haitian crisis by Patterson, a Rhodes scholar, was "unsophisticated." The gratuitous slight served only to deepen a belief widespread in the Caribbean that the United States, acting alone, had indeed, overthrown the government of a regional democratic neighbor.

48

U.S. State Department
Monday, March 1, 2004

W HILE PRESIDENT ARISTIDE AND HIS WIFE
were en route to an undisclosed destination and before the
unmarked American aircraft began its final approach to the Bangui
airport in the Central African Republic on Monday, March 1, American officials released a letter that they said had been written in
Kreyol and signed by the president sometime on Saturday, February
28. The United States embassy in Port-au-Prince translated what
they said was the letter's most important passage into English as:
"Tonight I am resigning in order to avoid a bloodbath."

Earlier on the same Monday, Mary Ellen Gilroy, director of the
Office of Caribbean Affairs at the State Department in Washington, placed a call to Dr. Bryant Freeman, a Kreyol language expert at
Kansas University in Lawrence, Kansas, and asked him to translate
the controversial "resignation letter of former Haitian President

Jean-Bertrand Aristide." Dr. Freeman, who at the time was working on the fifth edition of his 55,000-word Kreyol–English dictionary, said that Gilroy had called him because they had worked together before and she held in high regard his forty-five-year body of work in the field.

After studying the letter's Kreyol text, Dr. Freeman reported back to Gilroy that contrary to the claims of the U.S. embassy in Port-au-Prince, Aristide never wrote "I am resigning." Instead, he had written, "Thus, if this evening it is my resignation which can prevent a blood-bath, I agree to leave . . ."

He was *not* resigning. He was describing in Kreyol to the Haitian people the outer limits of how much in spilt blood they should reasonably be asked to pay for the preservation of their fragile democracy.

"If he (Aristide) were addressing the international community, he would use an international language either French or English," Dr. Freeman explained. "Creole (Kreyol) is the language of direct honest discourse between people in Haiti. He was trying to communicate with his people."

American officials had armed and directed the thugs, organized an unelected and unelectable opposition, and choked the Haitian economy into dysfunctional penury. Now the American secretary of state, Colin Powell, was saying around that his country's proxy killers would be coming south to scale the cordons that the people of Port-au-Prince had fashioned into crude ramparts in defense of the capital.

49

Miami International Airport
Saturday, March 13, 2004, 8:00 P.M. EST

W E ASSEMBLED IN THE DARKENED LOBBY OF
the airport hotel located inside the terminal building just off
the grand concourse of the Miami International Airport. It had been
two weeks since the Aristides had been forced from their home and
taken off to the Central African Republic. Three of us—Maxine
Waters, Ira Kurzban, and I—had spoken to either the president or
his wife by telephone almost daily. While we couldn't put a name to
it, we sensed that a countdown toward some unpleasant outcome had
begun.

Hours after arriving in the Central African Republic, Aristide, after describing to the media how he and his wife had been abducted
from their home by American soldiers, abruptly learned where the
sympathies of his African hosts lay: "The authorities have already
called on Aristide to remain calm, to stop making accusations against

217

America," said Foreign Minister Charles Wenezoui. "We fear that this kind of declaration compromises relations between the Central African Republic and the United States."

From what we could gather, President Bozize, who'd returned to the capital, Bangui, and received the Aristides after a three-day absence, had extended his guests an ambivalent measure of courtesy and leeway. He provided them with a telephone in their small two-room suite. He allowed them to attend church. He also allowed them to be taken for a short drive around the capital. Although the Aristides were not treated like prisoners, they were given no impression that they were free to take their leave of President Bozize's "care." Their unfree status was confirmed by French Defense Minister Michele Alliot-Marie, who said on the record that the Aristides were being guarded by French soldiers based in Bangui. Moreover, the Aristides were not informed by President Bozize, the former army general, of their ultimate fate. They were not even sure that *he* had yet been told by his American and French masters what that fate was to be. In any case, if anything had yet been decided, the Aristides had no inkling of it. Wearing the same clothes they had left Haiti in, they sat waiting in their rooms day after day, left to guess and to dread their fate.

During our last calls to them in Bangui, we said we would be coming to the Central African Republic to try and rescue them. Ira Kurzban made the arrangements for the plane on which we would be leaving at 9:00 P.M. The Central African Republic required visitors to arrive with visas. These would have taken weeks to secure from an embassy in Washington that was locked and shuttered much of the time, and so we decided to go without them.

I had read two advisories that the State Department had issued on the subject of travel to the Central African Republic. The first was dated April 7, 2003:

> The U.S. Department of State warns U.S. citizens against travel to the Central African Republic (CAR), and recommends that any Americans remaining in the country depart. On March 15, rebel forces that had been operating in the countryside outside Bangui took over the capital and seized power from the government of the CAR. The security situation throughout the country remains unstable.
>
> On November 2, 2002, the U.S. Embassy in Bangui suspended operations. There is no U.S. diplomatic or consular representation in the CAR. . . .

The second State Department advisory was issued almost a year later on February 13, 2004, two weeks before the abduction and delivery of President Aristide to the Central African Republic:

> The U.S. Embassy in Bangui is not currently open. . . .
> OTHER HEALTH INFORMATION: Malaria is prevalent in the Central African Republic. P. falciparum malaria, the serious and sometimes fatal strain found in CAR and many parts of Central Africa, is resistant to the anti-malarial drug chloroquine. . . . "

The Aristides had been detained in the Central African Republic for two weeks. Neither their American abductors nor their French and African captors had seen fit to provide them with antimalaria medication.

In a short while, we would take off to fly halfway round the world without proper travel documents to a destination that had been placed off limits to American visitors by the U.S. Department of State. We had no idea of how we would be received in Bangui, a place that none of us (who, with the exception of Ira Kurzban, were all well traveled in Africa) had ever visited. We had but two arrows in our quiver: an offer to the Aristides of temporary asylum from the government of Jamaica to be presented by Sharon Hay-Webster, and Maxine Waters, a member of the United States Congress. Still, during the long overnight flight, each of us would imagine something disastrous happening at altitude to the small plane in which we were riding across the Atlantic in tense, encapsulated silence.

The lobby of the Miami International airport hotel is appointed in what one could loosely call heavy-use-low-cost-moderne. The members of our party sat facing each other in a faux leather chair group situated amid the crowded foyer. Air travelers eddied past en route to a noisy bar in the adjoining room. On facing sofas next to us, a group of middle-age Italian men sang in a loud muscular alcohol-sodden competition of arias.

Waters sat quietly reading the asylum offer signed by P.J. Patterson, the prime minister of Jamaica. Sharon Hay-Webster, Patterson's emissary and a member of the Jamaican parliament, had shown the document to Waters and her husband, Sidney Williams, as well as to Ira Kurzban and myself, who were sitting across a large square coffee table from the three of them.

We were all but ready to make our way over to the general aviation terminal, where the plane had been readied for departure by its four pilots. Two of the pilots would fly the first leg of the trip while the other two slept. Our plan was to fly seventeen hours to Bangui, retrieve the president and his wife, and fly them back to Jamaica. With two planned outbound refueling stops, we could expect to arrive in Bangui by nightfall of the following day. We would then try to persuade President Bozize to allow President Aristide and his wife to leave the Central African Republic with us.

During his talks with the Aristides, President Bozize had nebulously characterized them as nonprisoners politely constrained to stay with him for a while. From what we could learn over the phone, they were being held in gentle detention or something of the dangerously unstable sort that one fears to have further defined until necessary.

Those of us involved in the rescue effort believed that the plan had been for President Aristide and his wife, Mildred, to die mysteriously in the *French-controlled* Central African Republic, perhaps of malaria, against which they had been provided no protection. Not knowing where they were being taken until the plane had begun its descent, the Aristides were never told about the grave dangers of contracting *P. falciparum malaria*, the sometimes fatal strain present in the Central African Republic. Their American abductors simply expelled them from the aircraft and left.

The French had done something like this to one of Haiti's leaders before:

> About the middle of May, 1802, *in the dead of night*, a ship of
> the line and a frigate anchored near Gonaïves, and landed a
> body of troops, which immediately surrounded the house
> of Toussaint, *who with his family was asleep*, and consequently,
> unconscious of his danger. Brunet, a Brigadier-General,

and Ferrari, aid-de-camp to Le Clerc, entered the hero's chamber with a file of grenadiers, and demanded his instant surrender. This was not a time for resistance. The lion was in the toils, and opposition was fruitless, and before any aid could be procured, the whole family, including the daughter of a deceased brother, were on board the frigate and under sail for France! Two Negro chiefs, who attempted to rescue their Governor [Toussaint], were taken, and afterwards shot while about a hundred of the confidential friends of Toussaint were arrested and sent on board different ships of the French squadron. From this imprisonment, they never returned, but were either sold as slaves on the coast of Barbary, or, what is more probable, thrown overboard and drowned.

"A Sketch of the Life of Toussaint L'Ouverture
The Haytian Patriot"
Oriental Herald
December 1828

On April 7, 1803, nine months before his army's final victory over France, Toussaint L'Ouverture, Haiti's founding father and revolutionary hero, froze to death in a jail cell high in the Jura Mountains of France three thousand feet above sea level.

● ● ●

With short notice, I had called Randall Pinkston of *CBS Evening News* and invited him to put together a television crew to go with us to Bangui. I had known Pinkston for many years and had once traveled in a delegation with him to Cuba. I held him in high regard. He was also black.

We had space on the plane for a television journalist and a camera person, as well as a print journalist.

We believed that including a journalist from a major American news organization would afford us a small measure of security against the fury of hard-nosed Bush administration operatives who were certain to be incensed over our direct and undisguised interference in the administration's foreign policy affairs.

I had discussed possible journalists with Maxine Waters, and we agreed that I should start by offering the story opportunity to a black television journalist and a black newspaper journalist. We anticipated, naïvely as it turned out, that there would be significant media interest, given the intense, if wrongheaded, coverage of the coup and the events leading up to it.

CBS turned down Randall Pinkston's request to go with us. I received much the same response from NBC, ABC, and CNN.

The television news networks were not interested.

I briefly considered calling the New York Times and then decided against it. The paper would almost certainly send Lydia Polgreen, the reporter who had described a bicentennial turnout of hundreds of thousands of Haitians at the National Palace as a "small but enthusiastic" gathering.

I then called Kevin Merida and Donna Britt at home in Takoma Park, Maryland. Kevin was an editor and Donna a columnist for the Washington Post. They were black, husband and wife, and friends of Hazel's and mine. Owing to fixed obligations, neither of them could go with us. Merida said, "I think the paper would be interested though. I'll work on it and call you back."

The night before our departure, I called Amy Goodman of Democracy Now at home. Goodman said, "I'm 90 percent certain. Let me call you back." Hours before my talk with Goodman, Merida called to tell me, "The *Post* would like to send Peter Eisner. He's a friend and a decent guy. You'll like him."

At about 11:00 P.M., an hour after I had spoken to Goodman, she called: "I'll meet you in Miami."

We were all but set. As we rose to walk from the hotel lobby toward the plane gate, an animated woman who looked to be in her thirties rushed up to me. She was out of breath from running. She wore an orange T-shirt draped loosely over rumpled jeans. She carried nothing in her hands.

"I'm Lydia Polgreen of the *New York Times*. I want to go with you." She caught her breath and waited for my answer. I was stunned—not just by her presence which had suddenly materialized unbidden, but more by the color of her skin. Lydia Polgreen was black.

"I'm sorry, Ms. Polgreen, but that will not be possible. All the seats on the plane have been taken except the two that the president and his wife will be sitting in."

I saw right away that she was not one to accept defeat easily. Imploringly, she said, "Mr. Robinson, there must be room for one more." I apologized but there was simply no room, no room at all. Then she said something along the lines of "but I'm from the *New York Times*. . ." I looked at her for a moment and then gave her what I thought she saw to be an opening.

"We only had space for two news people, Ms. Polgreen. They are right through there, in the restaurant—Amy Goodman of *Democracy Now* and Peter Eisner of the *Washington Post*. With my mention of the

Washington Post, she drew her features into an expression that suggested that I had just made her point.

I could see that she was far from giving up.

She likely knew who New York–based Amy Goodman was. She likely further had guessed from his name what Peter Eisner was *not*. She must have thought in desperation that the only thing left for her to do was to somehow use my own history against me—because she said something that seemed, coming from her, most improbable.

"You should be taking a black journalist with you."

"I agree, Ms. Polgreen. We tried to do that. We wanted a network person and a major newspaper writer. The networks turned us down. I spoke to Kevin Merida—you know Kevin don't you?—at the *Post*. I wanted a black writer from the *Post* but we couldn't make it work. Time was too short."

"I'm here, I'm ready to go."

Exasperated, I repeated what I had said earlier. "There is no space left, Ms. Polgreen. You're not suggesting that I give one of the two seats to you, are you?

The look on her face made clear that that was precisely what she was suggesting.

"Good-bye, Ms. Polgreen."

I remember at that moment thinking of the less than salubrious roles that Colin Powell and Condoleezza Rice had played in the dismantling of Haiti's nascent democracy, and the dragooning of its democratically elected president to a distant, perilously unstable place in the grip of a military dictatorship. Race was important to me, yes, but only a fool would believe it to be everything. Lydia Polgreen would not have come with us even if the plane were half empty.

50

Bangui, Central African Republic
Sunday, March 14, 2004, 6:00 P.M., local standard time

TS UNDERCARRIAGE BATHED GOLD BY THE SET-
ting equatorial sun, the little plane, after seventeen hours in the
air, descended quietly toward the geographic center of the vast
African continent. Below, the capital city of Bangui nestled on a
forested bank against a shimmering Oubangui River, which separated the Central African Republic from the Democratic Republic of
Congo to the southeast.

Once the French colony of Ubangi-Shari, the Central African Republic, a country the size of Texas with 3.5 million people, gained a
nominal independence from France in 1960 and since had suffered
nine coups, all executed or influenced by France, the country that had
remained firmly in control of the former colony's economic and security affairs.

Once the Central African Republic had the third largest rain forest in Africa. But most of its woodlands have long since been degraded by French-controlled foreign logging interests that exported vast tracts of the country's sapelli, ayous, and sipo timber back to Europe.

While the earth holds gold, uranium, and the diamonds that produce over 50 percent of Bangui's export revenues, little if anything of tangible value has filtered down to the country's people, some of the poorest in the world. For long stretches following independence, a succession of cash-strapped governments had scarcely been able to pay the country's civil service workforce. The landlocked state's political stability was further undermined by ethnic tensions the French encouraged between the Baya and the Banda, the two largest ethnic groups, and smaller groups like the Sara, the Nabandi, the Azande, and the Mbaka.

Though the Central African Republic was all but unknown to the outside world, its northern game parks for years had been fashionable stops for the wealthy European game hunters who had flocked there to shoot the country's fast-diminishing wildlife.

The lights marking the landing strip were all that we could make out as the little plane touched down in the gathering darkness. As we turned slowly around at the end of the strip, I glimpsed in the shadowy distance the outline of a small darkened terminal building. The cone of the taxiing plane's landing light outlined against the deepening gloom two French soldiers walking posts beneath shouldered rifles behind a chain-link enclosure we would later learn was a French military base that adjoined the airport grounds.

We stepped down from the plane and looked around. The Bangui airport was like no civil/commercial facility I had ever seen. There were no planes. No passengers. No civilian activity of any sort. The place had the blacked-out look and feel of a military garrison on war footing. It was as though we had dropped uninvited from the sky into some clandestine defense operation. Armed soldiers strolled in and out of the shadows. As many of them were French as were African. Disembodied voices speaking Sangho and French mingled in the opaque, close darkness.

We were received on the tarmac by officials who appeared neither happy nor annoyed to see us. We were treated *correctly*, which was more than we had any reason to expect, given that none of us bore a valid visitor's visa.

For the first time, I felt a small scratch of disquiet. Our objective had been to take off for Jamaica with President Aristide and his wife within six hours of our arrival. But almost immediately, budding misgivings gave place to a wave of troubling questions for which we had no answers. First, we knew next to nothing about the complex political and social culture of the Central African Republic. While I had studied and visited Africa for half a lifetime, I had never paid very much attention to the Central African Republic. I had studied and crammed in the days leading to our departure, but two weeks hadn't been nearly enough time to cover the subject. I (and I suspected the rest of us as well) was flying virtually blind. Second, none of us had any idea what President Bozize had been asked by France and the United States to do with President Aristide and his wife, or, for that matter what President Bozize had been promised by France and the United States as a quid pro quo for whatever it was that he was supposed to do with them. Undoubtedly some exchange of favors had been agreed to and we had no inkling of what the terms and conditions of the agreement were.

We did know, however, that President François Bozize, a former army chief of staff who'd lived in exile in France after his first foiled coup d'état, had, virtually one year to a day before our arrival, overthrown the democratically elected government of President Ange-Felix Patasse in a coup that was staged while President Patasse was out of the country. We also knew that since taking power, Bozize had unsuccessfully sought validation for his unelected military government from both the African Union and the United States.* But none of this told us anything about what Bozize, France, and the United States had agreed to with respect to the Aristides.

Were the Aristides prisoners? It was apparent that they were. As we walked between two columns of armed soldiers into the small terminal building, a second question crept into my thoughts: Were we now prisoners as well?

We were led into a crowded room where twenty or so people, apparently members of the local press, were gathered to hear us describe the purpose of our visit. Speaking on behalf of our group, Waters and Hay-Webster summed up our mission with straightforward economy. This of course followed several discreet welcoming remarks from the officials who'd come to the airport to receive us.

It had grown completely dark by the time our small motorcade started for Bangui and the presidential palace where the Aristides were being held in two second-story rooms in a wing of the palace. Our vehicles sped through the city under a police escort. Owing to the darkness, I had first thought the city's streets deserted. The street lights either had been turned off or were not working. Much of our

* In May 2005, a year and two months after our visit, François Bozize received more than 64 percent of the vote in the second round of presidential elections. The elections ended more than two years of military rule.

drive into the city led along a straight, wide boulevard. When the headlights of the minivan in which our group was riding washed up over the sidewalk, I was surprised to find a tree-lined walkway teeming with people standing about and talking in the dark. As I was looking at this, I remembered something that an African affairs expert had once said to me half-jokingly: African self-determination and sovereignty in the Central African Republic do not reach more than an inch deep into the country's soil. From the ground up, the country belongs, at least nominally, to its citizens. Beneath the surface, however—where the gold, the diamonds, and the uranium lie—the earth remains the property of France. This was told to me with some amusement, but apparently there is a kernel of truth to the story. For nowhere on earth could a contrast in human fortune have been more sharply drawn than here in the Central African Republic, where 50 percent of the population survives on subsistence agriculture wrung painfully from the earth that contains nearly unimaginable reserves of mineral riches.

Four young people talking animatedly in a group on the sidewalk seemed to materialize out of the impenetrable murk, only to disappear back into it as we went sweeping past with klaxons howling. As we hurried along, I thought that bringing the Aristides—a democratically elected Caribbean president and his Haitian American wife—here was someone's idea of power's sporting use. It was as if they—Powell, Rice, perhaps even Bush himself—giggling and guffawing together, had said, *I'll tell you what let's do. Let's scuttle them in CAR. I bet that'll shut his high-sounding mouth. Where? CAR. Where's that? What difference does it make? It's halfway around the world. He's always talking about his love of Africa, let's give him Africa. Chirac will just love it.*

Indeed the Aristides had expressed on many occasions a love for Africa. And, yes, the Central African Republic was in Africa. But the country didn't belong to the Africans who inhabited it but, for all practical purposes, to France.

Years before, I had heard much about the elaborate palace in Bangui, and none of it had been commendatory. Putting what I'd heard in context, virtually all of the stories written about Africa in the American press were unflattering. Almost never were there accounts of Africans doing the kinds of constructive but mundane life-building things—couples holding hands, children playing happily, students talking at school, parents coming home, preparing dinner—that people do all over the world, day in and day out.

The palace was not at all what I'd been given to expect. The building was quite unremarkable and looked less like a palace than like a medium-size office building with a center section framed between two wings, all of which were box-shaped and anonymous like thousands of similar structures that blight the urban landscape of contemporary America.

We were shepherded along the back side of one of the wings to an exterior stairway extending down to the ground from the second-story landing of a veranda that spanned the length of the wing. At the bottom of the stairway, we saw the president and Mrs. Aristide standing side by side in shadow waiting for us. Their faces wore small, guarded smiles. Tired and emotionally drained, they appeared, nonetheless, composed and dignified. They warmly greeted Maxine Waters, Sidney Williams, Ira Kurzban, and myself. We then introduced them to Sharon Hay-Webster, Amy Goodman, and Peter Eisner. The president was still wearing the clothes he had been wearing when he and his wife had been taken from their home at Tabarre two weeks before.

Standing unobtrusively on the margin of this extraordinary reunion in the dark at the stairway bottom were two or more of the Aristides' minders. They were watching and listening to the somewhat-wooden fellowship that one is forced to practice while trying to behave naturally under unnatural circumstances.

Upstairs in the Aristides' rooms, without Amy Goodman and Peter Eisner, the two journalists who had traveled to Bangui with us, we were joined by Frantz Gabriel, the helicopter pilot and eyewitness to the coup who would later testify publicly to what the American soldiers had done at 4:00 A.M. on February 29. Shortly after sitting down, we learned from the Aristides that, before our arrival, they'd been given reason to doubt that President Bozize would release them to travel with us to Jamaica.

We spent most of the next four hours in the Aristides' quarters waiting for a final decision, that as things turned out, was not President Bozize's to make.

51

I N THE TUMULTUOUS MONTHS THAT PRECEDED THE
assault and abduction in Haiti, the Aristide government had come
to believe that its problems with the United States were not
grounded on any American challenge to the legitimacy of Haiti's democracy. If anything, President Aristide and Lavalas, his party, were
too democratic for the Bush administration's political palate. In the
administration's eyes, Aristide was a populist.*

Historically, the United States had never trusted foreign leaders
who employed the ideas of populism in their programs of gover-
nance. American distrust of Aristide and his government grew with
every new school, housing project, hospital, and AIDS awareness
front that he opened in the teeth of the U.S.-imposed hemisphere-
wide financial embargo that, months before the coup, had brought
Haiti's economy to a virtual standstill.

---

* *Merriam-Webster's Collegiate Dictionary* defines a *populist* as "a believer in the
rights, wisdom or virtues of the common people."

From the beginning of Aristide's second term, it had been made plain enough that the United States would only be satisfied with the removal of his government from office.

What was happening was not new to the region, however.

There were a number of twentieth-century precedents for what the United States was presently doing to Haiti. In the early 1900s, the United States had forced the Dominican Republic to give Washington the power to collect customs revenues at the Dominican Republic's major ports. In 1911, President William Taft sent the marines to the Dominican Republic to protect the customs house. In 1916, President Woodrow Wilson sent the marines a second time to take over the government of the Dominican Republic. In 1915, U.S. troops were sent into Haiti. For the next twenty years, Haiti's customs revenues were turned over to the United States. The American occupation of the Dominican Republic lasted until the end of 1924 and coincided in part with President Wilson's occupation of Haiti.

In 1951, Jacobo Arbenz Guzman was elected president of Guatemala on a land reform platform. In addition to accelerating the land reform program of his predecessor, Juan Arévalo, Arbenz raised the minimum wage to $1.08 a day. In response to Arévalo's more moderate program for land reform, the World Bank cut off loans and the United States terminated military assistance to Guatemala. In 1954, the United States intervened directly and overthrew the democratically elected Arbenz government, ostensibly to "combat communism" in the region.

> In March 1954, the American secretary of state, John Foster Dulles, was successful in having the Organization of American States pass a resolution to the effect that the

control of the political affairs of any American state by the communist movement would be regarded as a threat to the political independence of the American States as a whole. With the passing of the resolution, the Central Intelligence Agency was given the go-ahead to undermine and topple the Guatemalan government.

ROSEMARIE E. STEWART
The United States in the Caribbean

Of course, there were communists in Guatemala just as there were communists in other Latin American countries and in the United States itself. There were, however, no communists in the Arbenz cabinet if any with control over the army or police force. In any case, it was commonly believed that the United States had overthrown the Arbenz government to advance the business interests of a single American company—the United Fruit Company, now called Chiquita Brands.

There were no communists to speak of in Haiti, save the Cuban doctors, and the Aristide government had been indisputably democratic. None of this had mattered, however, to the Americans.

Aristide had annoyed Haiti's monied white and light-skinned upper class in much the same way that Arbenz, by raising the minimum wage and prosecuting land reform, had annoyed American business interests in Guatemala half a century before. Transgressions of this sort had traditionally provoked American hostility. As with Arbenz, whether Aristide was democratic or not mattered little, if at all. Wealthy Haitians wanted Aristide out. For the United States, that had been all that really counted.

American decisionmakers only feign concern about world poverty. And they sustain the lament only so long as the pretense and its addictive, but useless, solutions are profitable, directly or indirectly, to American private interests.

Stripped down to its raw operational values, this is how America, unclad, sums out to the world. The remains of it—democracy for instance, the frontispiece, the spangle, the shiny surface of America—is mere surplusage. In reality, it figures little in the calculus of how America makes its friends or chooses its enemies. It is the pretty thing that you *see* dangled before you, the blinding chrome bumper, but not the real force that makes the behemoth go.

The force, the power plant, is *money*, the relentless campaign to capture it, and the God-invoked armed ruthlessness to keep it.

Aristide had annoyed *it*, armed only with the puny reed of democracy.

In a contest with America, the advantage had always been weighted against the reformist Aristide. The Americans knew everything that Aristide was endeavoring to accomplish while Aristide knew little, at the start, of the manifold measures that the Americans were taking, covertly and publicly, to undermine his efforts to lift his country's poor.

Even after the methodically staged economic strangulation, coup d'état, and abduction, the world would have to learn from officials of the Central African Republic that Bangui had been chosen as a detention venue *not* by Aristide but by France and the United States, countries whose officials had been saying that Aristide himself had chosen to go to Bangui.

Central African Republic officials also confirmed sometime after the coup that President Bozize had been contacted initially not by the United States and France, but by President Omar Bongo of Gabon. Apparently wishing not to be linked directly to Bozize's military dictatorship in the Central African Republic, the United States and France had asked President Bongo if he, acting as something of a cutout, would request on their behalf that President Bozize detain for them the democratically elected abductee of the United States. After American soldiers delivered President Aristide to President Bozize, Central African Republic officials confirmed that they had conferred with French and American officials on a daily basis about the details of Aristide's detention. They also confirmed that President Aristide was not free to leave the Central African Republic or even speak freely after Aristide's initial press briefing, which had caused his warders considerable chagrin.

For the United States and France, Omar Bongo was an ideal choice to do their bidding with President Bozize, the army general, who a year earlier had overthrown a democratically elected president in his own mineral-rich but cash-starved country.

Seventy-year-old Bongo had been president of Gabon, a small oil-exporting West African nation, for nearly forty years. Though Bongo himself was wealthy, his government from time to time had difficulty meeting its payroll.

In 2003, American lobbyist Jack Abramoff asked President Bongo to pay him $9 million to arrange a meeting with President George W. Bush. On May 26, 2004, three months after his call to President Bozize on behalf of the United States and ten months following Abramoff's offer, President Bush met with President Bongo in the Oval Office.

52

Presidential Palace, Bangui
Sunday, March 14, 2004, 7:30 P.M. local standard time

THE ORDEAL HAD BEGUN TO TAKE ITS TOLL, AS evidenced by the lengthening silences in the little room that was nearly as tall as it was long or wide. Nothing remained within our control.

All things considered, the president and Mrs. Aristide had borne up well enough, even though their customary grace may have required from them more energy than they had stores left to supply. As for the rest of us—Maxine Waters, Sidney Williams, Sharon Hay-Webster, Ira Kurzban, and I—the adrenaline that had fueled us for nearly twenty-four hours had lost its masking property. We were all bone-tired and had little choice but to sit in the little room and wait.

We sat on soft, off-white leather sofas that faced from four sides into the middle of the room. Gunshots could be heard through the window coming from the city, or someplace near the city that was as dark as it had been when we had raced through it earlier that night. Though I don't recall anyone saying as much, we all knew what the gunshots had meant: that the army general-cum-president had more on his mind than the Aristides and the people who came in the night to try and take them away.

The State Department, warning Americans not to visit, had described the Central African Republic as a dangerously unstable place. Yet a detail of nameless American soldiers had unloaded the president and his wife on the tarmac as if they were parcels, without so much as a single soldier stepping off the plane.

Roger Noriega, the assistant secretary of state who was handling matters for Secretary of State Colin Powell, said on ABC's *Nightline* that President and Mrs. Aristide had been taken to the Central African Republic because that was where they had asked to be taken. In a press conference held on Monday March 1, the day following the coup d'état, Defense Secretary Donald Rumsfeld dismissed President Aristide's claim of being abducted by American forces and questioned why "when President Aristide met with his Caricom colleagues during the stopover in Antigua, he said nothing of the kind to them."

Both Rumsfeld and Noriega were telling easily provable lies.

●　　●　　●

Our wait was segmented by periodic visits from President Bozize's ministers, two and three at a time. By 8:30, we were being visited for the third time. The ministers' message, however, had not changed: President Bozize is in the palace but a meeting with you will not be possible. We are terribly sorry but the president is busy and has no time for you this evening. Perhaps there will be time tomorrow. But, we insisted, we cannot stay until tomorrow; we must leave tonight in a matter of hours, at the very latest by midnight. One of the ministers then mentioned that the next day, March 15, was a national celebration, and the president had invited us to join him in marking the one-year anniversary of his government. We did not say what we were thinking: that an antidemocratic military coup by our own country had brought us there to rescue an *elected* president being detained by an *unelected* president, in cahoots with France at the request of *our* president. Now we were being invited to celebrate the anniversary of the military overthrow of a democratically elected president by a former army general and an ally of the moment to *our* president, a man who never missed an opportunity to extol the wondrously elastic virtues of "democracy."

We did not say any of this, however. Waters only remarked that we had to take off within an hour or so and we urgently needed to speak with President Bozize.

"We are sorry, Congresswoman, but this is not possible." This was how the third visit by the ministers to the room in which we sat waiting with President Aristide and his wife, Mildred, ended.

At 9:00 we received a fourth visit from a younger government official whom I remembered seeing at the airport. We sensed intuitively that he would try to help us when and if he could. He invited us to join the president's ministers for dinner on a large terrace that overlooked the city, which remained shrouded in darkness. The terrace was a short walk along an outside walkway from where we were waiting. Our initial response to the invitation was reflexively American, meaning that we were in a damn-all-form preoccupying hurry. Remembering our African manners and considering that in Africa invitations to share a meal are never falsely or insincerely extended, we all—the Aristides included—went along to dinner, where our hosts proved pleasant and gracious. The food was excellent.

During dinner something occurred to me that an assistant to Secretary of State Colin Powell had said on the phone a day or so before we left the United States: "Aristide is free to leave when he wants to."

I had thought at the time that Powell's assistant was bending the truth. But the Aristides had not been placed behind bars, just as our group had not been locked up following our unwelcome arrival. Indeed, we had been treated quite graciously. But there was no gainsaying the fact that the government of the Central African Republic was a military dictatorship, and while the Aristides may have been "free to leave," this did not mean that they *could* leave. Being here underscored and dramatized the distinction. By now, the seriousness of the Aristides' (and perhaps now even *our*) dilemma had finally come home to me. Having taken in what there was to see between the airport and the drive in to the palace—the gunshots, the blackout, the ubiquitous French and local soldiers, the hushed city, the general war security atmosphere—it dawned on me that *no one* could *leave* the Central African Republic without the active aid of the government.

Until the answer was *yes*, the answer was *no*.

Back in the room, 10:00 came and went without a visit from the ministers. We had all fallen quiet. President Aristide sat next to his wife on a sofa against an exterior wall. Looking pensive, he sat upright in his suit jacket with his legs crossed. The knot in his somber blue tie remained centered beneath the white collar of a dress shirt. Weary eyes betraying her natural composure, Mildred Aristide sat beside her husband in readiness. Across from them sat Waters and Williams. For a time, they seemed to have been staring deep inside themselves, their tired forms lightly touching. Ira Kurzban spoke inaudibly to Sharon Hay-Webster and then became quiet. Frantz Gabriel had left the room to collect something for the president.

In those silent, still moments, with no possible way to form an expectation of what was to come of us, I thought of Hazel with a sharp unnameable longing that felt not unlike grief.

By 10:15, we had been sitting in the room for the better part of three hours. Something had to happen, and soon. We all sensed that it was critically important that something be *made* to happen within the hour. Still, we were reluctant to risk making matters worse than they already were. We knew neither the political nor cultural terrain that we were treading. We may already have been offending without knowing it. Viscera socialized in America were of little reliable use to us here. We could *see* nothing. Powerful officials outside the little room in which we waited knew more than we about what was to happen next. For they were all talking to each other—from Bangui to Washington to Paris—dictating in terse, dry language the future of Haiti and the lives of two, if not eight—no—the lives of millions of innocent, unwitting people. I then considered the gratuitous suffering my country had occasioned for a defenseless people who had never caused a moment's pain to a single American.

Then I was ashamed. Ashamed of my country. Ashamed of official America, crouched cruel and hiding behind the curtain of public ignorance. Ashamed of the Colin Powells and the Condoleezza Rices who, steeled by unmerited prestige, took full advantage of an American civil rights movement they never participated in, to become their own people's most dangerous enemies.

At 10:30, the foreign minister made his first visit to the room and announced that the president had decided to receive three of us:

President Aristide and the two visitors who represented some measure of governmental authority—the congresswoman from the United States and the parliamentarian from Jamaica. Mildred Aristide was to remain in the little room with Sidney Williams, Ira Kurzban, Frantz Gabriel, and me.

53

Maxine Waters and Sharon Hay-Webster accompanied President Aristide to the center section of the palace and were ushered into a small office by the foreign minister. A man of medium height and build dressed in a gray suit, white shirt, and tie rose from a chair behind a small desk and nodded toward five chairs that had been placed in front of the desk.

The man was President François Bozize. He said nothing. Something, however, in his expression and demeanor signaled those who were sitting before him that this was a man to be taken seriously.

Wearing a steady neutral face—a military general's face—that was neither friendly nor unfriendly, President Bozize, speaking in French, acknowledged his petitioners, beginning with President Aristide. He then introduced three government ministers, the foreign minister and two others, including the young official we'd hoped would be helpful. Though President Aristide understood everything that President Bozize had said, Waters and Webster had not, and they looked toward President Aristide, who translated President Bozize's words into English, while the young minister would translate into French the brief appeal that Waters would make.

President Bozize finished his opening in a sure, quiet voice that was accustomed to being listened to. He then lifted his hands, turned his palms upward, and, with this small gesture, offered the floor.

Waters smiled appreciatively. The president continued with a face that betrayed nothing. The congresswoman began: "Mr. President, on behalf of all of us, I'd like to thank you for your hospitality, and for your treatment of President Aristide and his wife, Mildred Aristide. We have come to take them back to Jamaica. Prime Minister Patterson has agreed to have President Aristide in Jamaica. This is very important. Sharon Hay-Webster, a member of the Jamaican parliament, has brought a letter for you from Prime Minister Patterson offering to President Aristide temporary asylum in Jamaica."

Webster unfolded the letter that she had been holding in her hand and extended it across the desk to President Bozize.

President Bozize passed the letter to the young minister who translated it for him. President Bozize looked at Hay-Webster and nodded his understanding. He then shifted his eyes back to the congresswoman: "Do you have a letter from President Bush?"

For a long moment, the room was completely quiet.

"Mr. President, I do not represent President Bush. We are supportive of President Aristide, but this is not true of everybody in the United States."

For the first time, if only slightly, the president's expression changed. He looked down at his hands and then straight at Waters. He said two words in French. The meaning in his tone arrived before President Aristide's translation.

"Eh bien"—*well*—his voice marked with reluctance—he proceeded to confess what we already knew—that he had agreed to detain President Aristide as a favor to the French and the Americans.

"I would have to ask the French who asked me to let Aristide be here. I would have to ask the Americans. Without discussing it with them, I couldn't just let him go, you understand."

Waters tried to think of where to take the discussion next. Then President Bozize spoke again. "Maybe tomorrow, we can talk with some people."

"No, no, Mr. President, we have to leave tonight. No more than an hour from now."

Waters paused to wait for a response from President Bozize, who by then had grown visibly agitated. The room fell silent again. Waters looked at President Aristide sitting to her right, composed, self-contained. What a perilously absurd situation the United States had placed us all in! Aristide, a democratic president who'd been elected twice by the largest margins on record for free elections in the Americas; the former priest, lodestar to the poor whose country had twice the population of the Central African Republic. There the worthy man sat, waiting for, in fact *translating* for his captor, a military coup leader who held the democratically chosen president's fate in his hands, an army general who bore no particular ill will toward the Haitian democrat but nonetheless *needed* France in order to survive and *desired*, with a fever, America, in some unthought-out way, to help him, to recognize his government.

The general/president appeared to grow angry perhaps less with the *opportunity* that was fast turning into a problem, than with the two women across from him who were making it such. Stern-faced, he said, "What would I look like releasing President Aristide to two women who came here out of nowhere?"

Waters considered this for a moment and then threw caution to the wind: "I am a member of the United States Congress. I must be back in my office in Washington on Monday; therefore my colleagues and I must leave tonight."

She paused to put space between her sentences. She drew in a breath and said something, inaudible to the others, into the ear of the foreign minister who translated it for President Bozize, who became even more visibly upset.

"I am not doing that!"

"That's what they're going to think."

"Well, that is not true."

He took a moment and collected himself. "Look, I am not holding you but I have to make the right decision."

He paused again—somewhat longer this time. "You know we are trying to get some assistance from the World Bank. I don't want to do anything that is going to hurt us with the World Bank."

The dilemma—the fix in which we have *all* found ourselves for so long trapped—was circular, all-inclusive. Waters knew well what was happening to the gold, diamonds, and uranium. The tragedy of colonialism had not ended with the fiction of independence.

The congresswoman waited.

Then Bozize said somewhat resignedly, "Well, will you help us?"

"I don't know what I can do but I'll do what I can."

Closing the meeting before taking the matter of releasing President Aristide under advisement, President Bozize said, "This is very important. If you could help us to get the money from the World

Bank that we are negotiating for, that they are promising us, we would appreciate it."

●   ●   ●

At twelve midnight, six hours after our arrival, our plane lifted off from the Bangui airport with President Jean-Bertrand Aristide, his wife, Mildred Aristide, and the Haitian helicopter pilot, Frantz Gabriel, aboard. Relieved but drained, we were bound for Jamaica with intermediate refueling stops in Senegal on the West African coast and in Barbados, on the southeast side of the Caribbean archipelago.

54

Airborne, 35,000 feet above the
Central African Republic–Cameroon border
Monday, March 15, 2004, 1:00 A.M. local time

March 15, 2004

Dearest Hazel,

For some reason, our communication channel to you through Amy's operation in New York has gone down. We don't know why. In any case, I hope the problem is a temporary one. If it is not, I will have to wait until we reach Barbados to call you on Maxine's cell phone. Under the circumstsances, however, I thought the wisest course would be to write this letter to you now. I will entrust it to someone at the airport in Senegal to mail from there.

Before her signal went down, the indefatigable Amy broadcasted, I think from Bangui, what we have been able to accomplish. I am not sure that you have heard yet, but we were able to secure the release of Mildred and Titid. They are with us now onboard with Frantz Gabriel, the president's helicopter pilot. They, of course, are very tired but are otherwise in sound health.

It is 1:00 A.M. here. We took off from Bangui an hour ago. I do not know that "they" will allow us to get away with this. So long as we are over land, I feel relatively safe. Thus, I am confident that we aill be fine, at least as far as Senegal.

A few words about Bozize and the French situation here. Remember the poem about colonial British Guiana by Martin Carter, entitled *This is a dark time, my love.*

> *It is the season of oppression, dark metal and tears.*
> *A festival of the guns, the carnival of misery.*

Well, this sums up the painful dilemma of much the whole of the black world in its relationship to much the whole of the white world. Perhaps it is fatigue speaking, but it would seem that little of consequence has changed in the way that the white world behaves towards out countries. It cannot be gainsaid that "independence" for them is little more than a mean fiction.

They still endeavor to manipulate us, as if they still owned us, and I suppose if they can manipulate us so easily and successfully, they do, in fact, still maintain control of, at least, our most important facility—our minds. Consider, paticularly in this case, the disgraceful examples of Powell and Rice.

Although I know little about Bozize other than that he gained "power" via a military coup, he, at least in one way, finds himself in a tough spot—that of small real power, with either no choices, or, bad choices. The French still own and run this place, just as they believe themselves, two hundred years after the Haitian Revolution, to still own Haiti. Clearly, the Americans, the French, the Canadians, the British, the Australians and all the world's other white people regard our Presidents, whether they are democratically elected or not, as toy presidents and our countries as toy countries. This is the galling infuriating nub of the matter. Maybe, I am giving this opaque general more credit than he is due, but perhaps Bozize saw this as the tiny sliver of common ground he shared with Titid.

In CAR at the airport, as we were leaving with Mildred and Titid, a French soldier stared at me with a hateful intensity. For a moment, I thought that we had read each other's minds. He looked to be little more than a child. Something about his aspect, however, something he took as an article of faith, seemed to enlarge him, as if he were, alone and peering out of the dark, a vested sentinel dispatched to the provinces with orders to defend the empire. He obviously had never gotten the bulletin. Or was it we who hadn't gotten it.

This is enough for now. I've lost track of the time and the days. I can't remember when I last slept. I am going to try now.

I'll tell you everything when I get home.

I love you very much.

Randall

P.S. Maxine has demonstrated extraordinary courage and boldness here.

55

National Parliament Building, Port-au-Prince, Haiti
Sunday, May 14, 2006, 11:40 A.M. local time

MANY OF THE FOREIGN DIGNITARIES SPRINKLED among the guests attending the May 14 inauguration of Rene Garcia Préval at the parliament seemed not to divine the obvious. Taken as a whole, with the *whole* including conspicuously the peasantry, the Haitian people were somehow different from other blacks in the postslavery West. They alone evinced a peculiarly tenacious self-possession that many of the dignitaries present hoped had departed the country with deposed president Jean-Bertrand Aristide. They had, of course, spotted the annoying trait in him, and had thought, perhaps out of arrogance or simple ignorance, that the *problem* extended no further. After all, the *problem* had brought the country only grief. Surely everyone had had enough of that.

Préval, unlike Aristide, was not a scintillating orator. The sixty-three-year-old agronomist, who had served a term as president between Aristide's two abbreviated terms, was by nature a quiet man.

With the country bridling under a foreign occupation managed by Washington, Paris, and Ottawa, Préval, according to the Provisional Electoral Council's count that many believed was understated, had emerged from a field of thirty-four candidates with 51 percent of the vote. Guy Philippe, the former Delmas police chief and leader of the paramilitary force of thugs armed and directed by the United States, received 1.92 percent of the vote, while Charles Henri Baker, a wealthy mixed-race businessman and brother-in-law to Andy Apaid, the leader of Group 184, was said to have received 8.24 percent of the vote.

The inaugural ceremony had been organized by the unelected interim government the United States had installed following Aristide's abduction more than two years before. Under orders from the United States, France, and Canada, the interim government had banned Aristide from returning to his homeland from South Africa, where he, with his wife and two daughters, had been living in exile for nearly two years since leaving Jamaica under pressure from Washington.*

Florida governor Jeb Bush was on hand that sunny May morning for the swearing-in of Haiti's new president. The governor was representing his brother, George W. Bush, the abductor/president who had once lost his own nation's presidential popular vote but had become

* The Jamaican government had warned from the beginning that it would not be able to withstand American pressure for more than two to two and a half months. As President and Mrs. Aristide waited in Jamaica to go to South Africa, Reverend Jesse Jackson called Hazel and me to propose that Aristide ask the U.S. government for asylum. Such an offer from the United States would have been seen as evidence in support of Secretary of State Colin Powell's specious claim that the Bush administration played no role in the coup. What's more, an Aristide acceptance of an American asylum offer would have satisfied two further Bush administration objectives: first, Aristide would have been discredited in the eyes of the large majority of Haitians, who had twice elected him president, and, second, he would have been placed under the American administration's direct control.

president in spite of that, after being gifted with Florida's twenty-five electoral votes by the Supreme Court of the United States.

After his brother's abduction of Aristide, Jeb Bush, whose state election officials had blocked thousands of blacks in Florida from voting against his brother, was to say pharisaically of the kidnapped Haitian president: "Democracy means more than elections. It means respecting the rule of law and supporting a vibrant, robust civil society. Aristide destroyed these principles in Haiti and replaced them with corruption and violence. Groups such as the Congressional Black Caucus who claim to support democracy yet focus on Aristide's election, exacerbate his betrayal of the Haitian people.

"Haitians, now free of Aristide's grip, can begin rebuilding their country and reclaiming their future. . . . (Gérard) Latortue's appointment (by the United States) as interim prime minister of Haiti reflects a commitment to the honest, effective leadership required to guide Haiti forward to stability, democracy, and success."*

If the Florida governor saw irony in his remarks, it was not apparent.

Though Latortue, a Haitian émigré based in Boca Raton, had excluded the new president's ordinary supporters from the inaugural ceremony, chants from Préval's supporters penetrated from outside the room and bounced around its walls.

"Tie up Latortue! Tie up Latortue! Tie up Latortue!"

The chants grew louder as the proceedings wore on. On this august occasion, sitting among the midrank foreign diplomatic glitterati, La-

---

* In an early act of office, Latortue rescinded the application made the year before by the deposed democratic Haitian government for restitution from France. The demand was for the $21 billion Haiti had been forced to pay in reparations to France following the successful slave revolt. For this and other favors rendered by Latortue to the United States and France, Florida Republican Representatives Mark Foley and E. Clay Shaw Jr introduced on July 24, 2006, House Resolution 941, "Honoring the service of Gerard Latortue, Haiti's interim prime minister."

tortue, a retired World Bank apparatchik, desperately hoped to escape the personal embarrassment that came with being shouted at through the windows by his own people. Though he was not surprised that they disliked him so, or even that they looked on him as something of a traitor or an American puppet, he dreaded being made a spectacle of on this historic day he imagined himself to have brought about.

The new president began his remarks, "Welcome to Her Excellency, the Honorable Michaelle Jean, governor-general of Canada. Welcome to His Excellency, the Very Honorable Perry Christie, prime minister of the Bahamas; His Excellency, Richard Tauwhare, governor of Turks and Caicos; His Excellency Jose Alencar, vice president of Brazil; His Excellency Jose Vincente Rangel Veca, vice president of Venezuela; Mr. Philippe Douste Blazy, foreign minister of France; Mr. Carlos Morales Troncoso, foreign minister of the Dominican Republic; Mr. Bernandino Leon, foreign minister of Spain; Mr. Jeb Bush, governor of State of Florida. . . . "

Outside, the demonstrators ratcheted up the volume.

"Tie up Latortue! Tie up Latortue!"

The demonstrators, numbering in the thousands, were moving between the Cathedral, the National Palace, and the Parliament building where the corpulent and motionless form of Gérard Latortue sat mortified—amid emissaries that included many from countries that had played important roles in the coup d'état.

Préval, a soft-spoken, distinguished-looking agronomist, carried on with his remarks, "Welcome to all other representatives of peasants, presidents, and heads of governments, the representatives of foreign parliaments. . . . "

"Tie up Latortue! Tie up Latortue! Tie up Latortue!"

The chants were increasing in volume and pace. Many in the clamorous crowd outside wore green and yellow T-shirts with Préval's picture on them. Although they were members of Préval's Espwa party, they held high above their heads posters and pictures of Aristide.

The crowd began a new chant.

"Whether they like it or not! Aristide is returning! Whether they like it or not! Aristide is returning!"

One of the demonstrators, an unemployed twenty-six-year-old laborer from Martissant named Claude, said, "We voted for Préval on February 7, 2006, so that Aristide could return. We have come here to support Préval. But we say to Préval he must get tough so that Aristide can return to the country."

Inside the parliament chamber, Governor Jeb Bush, the abductor/president's brother and emissary, sat two seats down from José Vincente Rangel, the vice president of Venezuela. The two men did not shake hands or speak.

Boniface Alexandre was the accommodating and easily operable old judge who had served all but invisibly as president in the U.S.-installed interim government of Haiti. Tradition required that the outgoing president present the presidential sash to the newly elected president. When called on to perform the ceremonial task, President Préval gave his back to the unelected Alexandre and accepted a substitute presidential sash from Joseph Lambert, president of Haiti's Senate and a member of President Préval's Espwa coalition.

"Inauguration 2006: Giant Crowds Hail Préval and Demand Aristide's Return"

... during the VIP reception in the Parliament's Senate lounge immediately following the swearing-in, Préval refused to have his photo taken standing between Alexandre and outgoing de facto Prime Minister Gérard Latortue, preferring to stand to their side.

Haiti Progrès
May 17–23, 2006

The chants coming from the street were as loud as ever.

"Tie up Latortue! Tie up Latortue!"

"Whether they like it or not! Aristide is returning! Whether they like it or not! Aristide is returning!"

Between February 29, 2004, the day of the abduction, and May 14, 2006, the day of President Rene Préval's inauguration, an estimated four thousand Haitian men, women, and children were killed by the American-armed thugs, the interim government's national police force, as well as by American, French, Canadian, and United Nations troops. On the day of the inauguration, however, the Haitian commonalty appeared to have lost none of its tenacity and determination.

Although United Nations forces tried to keep the mobile crowds from assembling in front of the National Palace, the mass of people eventually overcame the pepper spray, broke through the military barricades, and took over the street.

Although the police and U.N. Mission to stabilize Haiti (MINUSTAH) had established a ban on all vehicles in the vicinity of the Parliament, Cathedral and (National) Palace, the street leading from the Cathedral to the Palace, was choked with masses of people. In front of the Palace, hundreds of U.N. troops—grouped in national contingents from China, Nigeria, Senegal, Pakistan, Benin, Brazil, etc—held back a boisterous sweating sea of humanity. . . . The musical animation that blasted through the giant banks of speakers set up on the Palace lawn had a timidly anti-coup theme which pleased the crowd assembled outside the gates. Many sang along with the songs. An emcee at one point saluted the people of Cité Soleil for their "resistance."

Ironically, however, most of the people in the (Palace) stands were the government officials and politicians which backed the 2004 coup and kidnapping of Aristide. Many in the throngs in front of the Palace, which eventually pushed their way through the lines of the Haitian police and U.N. troops up to the Palace fence, resented that the people who voted Préval in were outside the gates while the coup backers were inside. "Those who used to kill us, who used to try to prevent Préval from becoming President, are inside!" Marline Joinville, twenty, told Reuters.

"The bourgeoisie want to hijack the president!" another demonstrator, Lesly Cherubin, told Reuters. "They are all over him while we, who elected him, can't even see him!"

Haiti Progrès
May 17–23, 2006

Later in the afternoon, after President Préval completed his address to the nation on the grounds of the National Palace, he turned and walked to where Jose Vincente Rangel Veca, the vice president of Venezuela, was sitting within two feet of Governor Jeb Bush of Florida. Without acknowledging Bush, the abductor/president's brother, President Préval took the vice president's hand and led him off to a conference room on the second floor of the National Palace.

There the two men addressed the international press corps. President Préval spoke first. "Today, we are signing with Venezuela the Petrocaribe accord. At 7:00 A.M. this morning, already 100,000 barrels of oil arrived in Port-au-Prince. We know what kind of relations there have been between Haiti and Venezuela. In Jacmel (Haiti), (Francisco de) Miranda created the Venezuelan flag and received aid from Haiti from President (Alexandre) Pétion. And the alliance was so strong that today at the foot of the stairs to (Venezuela's) National Palace, one finds two busts: one of Pétion and the other of (Simon) Bolivar."

Then Vice President Rangel spoke. "With this act, Venezuela pays a historic debt to Haiti. An eternal debt, which is also the root of liberty and the root of the Venezuelan nation. It is a debt not only to President Pétion but also to the thousands and thousands of Haitians who fought alongside Miranda for the liberty of not only Venezuela but of all Latin America. . . . We do not cultivate rhetoric. We do what is practical and concrete. We believe that solidarity means concrete acts."

By the time the two men completed their remarks, Governor Jeb Bush, the abductor/president's brother, had reached the airport and was on his way back to the United States.

Looking back on the election that returned Préval to office for a second term, one wonders whether or not American officials, leading up to the elections, forgot for a moment who Rene Préval really was. After all, his nickname was Twin, a sobriquet that described his philosophical resemblance to Aristide. It wasn't as if the United Nations and interim government officials hadn't tried to diminish Préval's chances of winning. They had done that by dramatically reducing the number of polling stations in poor areas. But the ploy had not worked. Nor had the United States experienced any success in influencing the political temperament of Haiti's recently enfranchised black poor. The poor knew what they wanted and that was that. For many, if not most of them, a vote for Préval was a vote for Aristide.

Indeed, everyone—the Americans, the French, the Canadians, the armed thugs, the rich, the Convergence politicians—*knew* what couldn't be said out loud for the public record: the "problem" was not Aristide or Préval or anyone else the majority of Haiti's people might elect to represent them. The "problem" was the very idea of democracy itself.

All of those involved knew perfectly well—particularly those making up the American-contrived Haitian opposition—that were Haiti to hold a thousand free and fair elections, the poor, on each and every occasion, would carry the day. Invariably they would choose someone who cared about their plight, someone who would, at the very least, provide them with a small chance for a less painful existence.

Aristide understood his opponents, the putschists, well enough: "They fear the principle of one man, one vote. They don't fear me; they fear the people. And they don't fear the people because the people are violent. They fear the people because the people are ready to vote."

This was the American dilemma in a nutshell. Yet again, *democracy* would be the petard on which powerful but hypocritical American officials would find themselves obliviously hoisted.

Though Rene Préval had won back the presidency, those who elected him did not delude themselves into believing that they had won back their democracy. The streets of the country were still patrolled by United Nations occupation forces, the same forces that had carried out several massacres in the period following the coup d'état. Guy Philippe and Louis-Jodel Chamblain remained free to come and go as they pleased. The interim government's police force, which had been responsible after the coup d'état for a spree of systematic killings, had yet to be reorganized.

At the inauguration ceremony, seated in a place of honor next to emissaries from the nations that had carried out and helped facilitate the coup, was former Haitian army general Prosper Avril. During his rule over Haiti, the ruthless military dictator made lurid public displays of political opponents he had tortured, parading their battered bodies before television cameras.

Only a few feet from General Avril sat Governor Jeb Bush of Florida, the state in which a U.S. District Court judge had found General Avril's military regime to have engaged in "a systematic pattern of egregious human rights abuses" and awarded six of the general's torture victims $41 million in compensation.

Sadly, real *democracy* remains a long way off for Haiti. For how can any reasonable observer contend to the contrary as long as foreign powers, directly or indirectly, remain bent on preventing Jean-Bertrand Aristide, Haiti's most widely respected humanist and democrat, from returning home to his own country.

●　　●　　●

Did the American press conspire with the Bush administration to cover up what actually happened to President Aristide, his American-born wife, and his democratic government? I'm perfectly happy to accept that there was no conspiracy as such. I take this view for two practical reasons. First, a conspiracy cannot be easily proved. Second, and more important, nothing much turns on whether or not

American policymakers *consciously* planned with news organizations to cover up what transpired before and during the early morning hours of February 29, 2004. After all, the American newsmakers and newscasters had little need to. They were all born into a narcissistic national culture of self-worshipers who take sustenance and reinforcement from looking on those who look or live or think or worship differently from themselves as inferior and thus worthy of ridicule, if not a good thumping or, worse, eradication, if one listens to the likes of Reverend Pat Robertson, the American televangelist who remarked that the assassination of President Hugo Chavez of Venezuela would be a good idea.

It is clear to me that the instinct of a great many, if not most, Americans is to praise themselves, even while attempting on occasion to practice a mild form of *praiseworthy* self-criticism. As if to inoculate themselves against serious self-criticism, they vaccinate themselves from time to time with a mild dose to ward off meaningful attacks of painstaking self-examination.

President Aristide, the democratically elected president of a country of 8 million people, claimed that he and his wife were kidnapped and taken to the Central African Republic by American soldiers. After finding them in Bangui being held against their will, I was certain that President Aristide had been telling the truth about what the soldiers had done. That being the case, the soldiers had committed an egregious wrong, at the very least, in Aristide's case, and probably several domestic felonies in his wife's case, owing to her being an American citizen.*

---

* On January 9, 2007, Congresswoman Barbara Lee (D-CA) introduced in the United States House of Representative H.R. 351 calling for the establishment of a commission "to examine and evaluate the role of the United States Government in the February 2004 coup d'etat in the Republic of Haiti."

Why did American news organizations fail to investigate Aristide's allegations? This was one of several questions that American journalists never bothered to raise or answer.

There were other questions as well.

Why were the armed paramilitaries that had torn a swath across the north of Haiti waiting in Gonaïves and not attacking Port-au-Prince at the time of the coup d'état?

Why had the American public been given to believe that the paramilitaries carried out the overthrow of the democratic government when the paramilitaries were far from Port-au-Prince at the time?

Where had the paramilitaries gotten the American weapons, ammo, bulletproof vests, grenade launchers, M50 machine guns, uniforms, boots, and steel pots?

What had the United States done to bring the Haitian economy to its knees in the years, months, weeks, and days before the night of the abduction of the president and his wife?

In the hours before their departure from Haiti with the paramilitaries far to the north, why did the Aristides work all day Saturday, February 28, to complete arrangements for two television interviews with American journalists Tavis Smiley and George Stephanopoulous, which were to be conducted on Sunday at the National Palace, if the Aristides had already decided to leave Haiti the day before?

With the paramilitaries in Gonaïves and the president under no immediate threat, why would the president and his wife *choose* to go with the American soldiers halfway around the world to the Central African Republic, instead of to Jamaica or Venezuela or another nearby country where they knew officials who would receive them?

Why were no pictures taken or film shot of the Aristides leaving their home or boarding the unmarked American plane?

Why were customs officials in Antigua not allowed to board the plane or learn who was on it?

Why had the customs declaration, given by the plane's American operators to Antiguan officials, been altered from showing that there were fifty people onboard (which accords with Frantz Gabriel's account) to showing that the plane carried *no* passengers?

Why did Defense Secretary Donald Rumsfeld lie about President Aristide meeting with Caribbean officials in Antigua when the president met with no one in Antigua—a country the president hadn't known he was even in?

Why were the Aristides not permitted to raise the plane's window shades that ground officials in Antigua verified were drawn?

Why were the Aristides never told where they were, or where they were being taken?

Why were the Aristides detained in the Central African Republic (a detention I witnessed firsthand) if they had chosen, of their own free will, to go there?

Why did Assistant Secretary of State Roger Noriega lie about this on ABC's *Nightline?*

Why did the American newspapers and television networks, which misleadingly described the role and whereabouts of the paramilitaries before the coup, all but cease their coverage of the Haitian crisis once the president and his wife had been taken to the Central African Republic under suspicious circumstances?

Why was such intense American television coverage given to antidemocratic paramilitary leaders like Guy Philippe and Louis Jodel Chamblain, who were little more than expendable American tools, and so little coverage given to the real local force and American ally behind the coup, Andy Apaid, a wealthy white American sweatshop owner the *New York Times* described as "a wealthy Haitian businessman," leaving the clear but wrongheaded impression that Apaid was a black Haitian when he was neither black nor Haitian?

Why was the American-installed prime minister, Gérard Latortue, shown after the coup by the Trinity Broadcasting Network grinning and groveling to American viewers for a used ambulance and fire truck, while Haiti's dignified constitutional prime minister, Yvon Neptune, languishing in a Haitian jail without charge or trial, remained—and remains—all but ignored by the American press?

There are other cases of postcoup human rights abuses every bit as compelling as Prime Minister Neptune's. Father Gerard Jean-Juste was for many years a strong advocate of Lavalas's social justice programs. Consequently the party urged him, after February 29, to enter Haiti's presidential election in order to continue the momentum for true democracy and social justice. Had he been allowed to run, he almost certainly would have swept the polls. To stop him, heavily armed masked men sent by Latortue's American-backed government surrounded his church while the priest was feeding six hundred children in his Parish of St. Claire one morning. They beat and handcuffed the priest to the screams of the terrified children. They dragged him through a shattered window. Threw him in jail. Accused him of importing arms and harboring gunmen. They then arrested him again, accusing him of committing a murder in Haiti while he, at the time of the murder, was in Florida. He was jailed in deplorable conditions that caused his health to deteriorate and was diagnosed with leukemia. Haiti's foreign-backed government kept him locked away for almost two years, until an international outcry secured his release for medical treatment.

Soeur Anne is a beloved Haitian folk singer, community activist, and Lavalas stalwart. Shortly after foreign troops dismantled Haiti's democracy, Soeur Anne's gate was blown away with explosives in the dead of night by troops sent by the foreign-backed Latortue government. Everyone in her house, including a five-year-old child, was hooded, handcuffed, and dragged off to jail by heavily armed men where she remained uncharged and untried until she was finally released by the new Préval government.

Two years following the abduction and coup, over four thousand Haitians are similarly being held without charge or trial by a government installed by the United States, France, and Canada. Why has virtually no attention been paid to this by the American media?

How would American media have treated the story had American soldiers abducted the president of a democracy that was comparable in size to Haiti, such as Greece or Austria or Belgium or Denmark?

Why did the American press, in Haiti's case, acquit itself so disgracefully?

●　　●　　●

Lastly, the evidence decisively showed that the United States, with the assistance of France, methodically undermined the political and economic stability of Haiti before abducting its democratically elected president and overthrowing its democratically elected government.

Owing to an extreme imbalance of power and influence between the small middle-income democratic countries of the Caribbean region and the large industrialized nations of North America and western Europe, calls from Caribbean leaders for an official investigation of the events of the early morning hours of February 29, 2004, were ignored.

The people of the democratic Caribbean were forced, due to their ironic proximity to *democratic* America, to accept certain unpleasant realities.

As between the big and small (i.e., the rich and poor) nations of the world, there exist *no* checks and balances. No fair panel of last resort, no higher court before which to petition for recourse, no hierarchy of enforceable rights, no scheme of natural equity or fairness. As long as one member nation of the global family of nations is free to behave toward a fellow member nation with lethal impunity—to bully, to menace, to invade, to destabilize politically or economically, to reduce to tumult—no country, so threatened, can hope to enjoy the social and political contentment that ought inherently to attend democratic practices.

Since Haitian slaves won their independence from France in 1804, the United States has loomed over Haiti like the sword of Damocles. The record of this abuse of power is well-known to the steadfastly democratic, English-speaking Caribbean nations that have little choice but to heed the chilling implications of this for their own survival. Their leaders have learned the hard way that, within their well-managed tropical island-states, no election verdict, no constitutional custom or habit, no parliament's decision, no ordinary citizen's commonplace democratic prerogative is safe from an intrusive hegemonic America whose caprices and policies are neither fairer, nor more predictable, nor more morally conscionable than the vagaries of hurricanes.

AUTHOR'S NOTE

The foregoing account of the American abduction of President Jean-Bertrand Aristide and his wife, Mildred Aristide, is constructed of events that I either participated in or was informed of by one or more firsthand witnesses whose statements were corroborated by others.

Most of those with whom I spoke feared reprisals and asked that their names not be divulged. Though some have remained in Haiti, others, if not most, have left the country.

Some interviewees agreed to go on the record.

In October 2005, I interviewed President Aristide and his wife over a five-day period in Pretoria, South Africa. During the course of that week, I also interviewed, extensively, Frantz Gabriel, the Haitian helicopter pilot who, along with a number of Haitian security personnel, witnessed the abduction of the President and his wife from their home in Tabarre.

I also spoke with Congresswoman Maxine Waters and Prime Minister Ralph Gonsalves of St. Vincent and the Grenadines.

My account of President Aristide's ruminations in the days before the coup was extrapolated from discussions I had with him in South Africa.

With the exception of one circumstance, every coup-related event described in this book is based on personal witness, the firsthand observation of others that I interviewed, or historical documentation. For obvious reasons, I suppose, I did not visit the camp of the American-armed paramilitaries who were readying in the Dominican Republic to overthrow the government of Haiti. Hence I could only guess at what these men were doing, thinking, and saying. For this short section of the narrative, I borrowed from my own experience as an infantryman in the United States Army.

ACKNOWLEDGMENTS

I owe a debt of gratitude to a great many brave people whose names cannot be published here. An even greater debt is owed to those who have consistently committed themselves to a public telling of what happened at American hands to Haiti's fragile democracy in the early morning hours of February 29, 2004. At the top of that list are President Jean-Bertrand Aristide and his Haitian-American wife, Mildred Aristide. Thanks, also, to Frantz Gabriel, who was present during the abduction and saw firsthand what the president, his wife, 7,500 elected government officials, and the Haitian people were yet again caused to endure.

I should further like to thank Chris Greenberg, my editor, whose recommendations proved immensely useful.

My narration of what happened in Haiti, before and after the coup d'etat, is enormously enhanced by the photographs that were made available to me by Amy Goodman of *Democracy Now*; Michelle Karshan, former foreign press liaison at the National Palace in Haiti;

Kevin Pina, film-maker and journalist; and Evens Sanon of the Haiti Dream Keeper Archives. I continue to appreciate the ongoing contributions of Marie Brown, my literary agent, who believed in this project and found a publisher who thought the work worth bringing to life.

I am also grateful for the meticulous time-consuming work of Jacqueline Bryan who typed the handwritten manuscript.

Lastly, I wish to thank my wife, Hazel, who has been for twenty-five years, my all and everything—kindred spirit, collaborative partner, helpful critic, and loving soul mate.

Randall Robinson can be reached at rr@rosro.com

INDEX

273